BACK-END DEVELOPMENT Unleashed

Techniques and Best Practices

Kiet Huynh

Table of Contents

CHAPTER I
Introduction to back-end development

1.1 What is back-end development?

Back-end development refers to all the behind-the-scenes activities that support the user-facing front-end of a software application. As a back-end developer, you are responsible for building and maintaining the server-side logic, infrastructure, databases and services that power the front-end experiences of a website, app or any other software product.

In a typical web or mobile application, the front-end consists of the client-side code written in languages like HTML, CSS and JavaScript that runs on the user's browser or mobile app. The front-end is focused on building intuitive and appealing user interfaces and experiences.

The back-end, on the other hand, consists of the server-side code written in languages like Java, Python, Ruby, C# etc. The key responsibilities of the back-end include:

- Developing APIs and microservices that enable front-end clients to fetch or mutate data and trigger business logic. Common architectures involve building RESTful APIs using JSON for data exchange.

- Managing data persistence using relational databases like MySQL or NoSQL databases like MongoDB. This includes defining data models and database schemas, writing optimized queries and configuring database servers.

- Implementing authentication, authorization and overall application security by using encryption, tokens, access controls etc.

- Building robust server infrastructure on top of frameworks like Express, Django, Rails, Spring etc. This includes setting up web servers, caching layers, queues for background jobs etc.

- Monitoring application performance, logs and errors to enable troubleshooting and prevent outages.

To summarize, the front-end focuses on the UI while the back-end focuses on the behind-the-scenes "engine" that powers the app. While front-end code runs on the client, back-end code runs on the server.

A real-world analogy would be a restaurant. The cooks and chefs work in a back kitchen to prepare the food, while the servers interact with customers directly to take orders and serve the prepared dishes. Just like the kitchen powers the restaurant, the back-end powers the front-end.

1.2 Role of back-end in web and mobile apps

The back-end serves as the foundation and engine for both web and mobile applications. While the front-end UI enables the user interactions, the back-end handles everything from data storage and processing to business logic to security.

Some key roles of the back-end in web and mobile apps include:

Data Persistence and APIs

The back-end provides mechanisms for saving and retrieving data in a persistent manner. Relational databases like MySQL and NoSQL databases like MongoDB are used to store and organize data. The back-end provides APIs for the front-end to perform CRUD (Create, Read, Update, Delete) operations on this data.

For example, a blogging app would use a database to store blog posts and metadata. The front-end website or mobile app can use REST APIs built on the back-end to load posts, create new posts, update posts etc.

Business Logic Implementation

Complex business logic such as payment processing, data validation, notifications, analytics etc. are all handled by the back-end. The front-end simply invokes APIs exposed by the back-end to trigger such logic.

For instance, the front-end of an e-commerce app would call a ChargePayment API when the user completes a purchase. The actual payment processing happens on the back-end servers.

Integration with Other Systems

The back-end acts as the integration layer between the front-end and other systems like payment gateways, shipping APIs, ad networks etc. This enables building composite apps by combining different services.

For example, an e-commerce app could integrate with PayPal or Stripe for payments, FedEx for shipping, Google Ads for promotions etc. all on the back-end.

Security and Access Control

Robust security mechanisms like encryption, access controls, tokens, rate limiting etc. are implemented by the back-end. The front-end simply leverages identity and access management APIs from the back-end.

For example, user authentication is typically handled by the back-end by issuing JWT tokens on successful login requests from the front-end.

In summary, the back-end provides the core frameworks and infrastructure that enables the front-end to focus purely on the user experience. The division of responsibilities between front and back-end allows rapid iterations on the front-end while the back-end remains stable.

1.3 Comparison of front-end vs back-end

While front-end and back-end development go hand in hand in building full-stack applications, they entail very different scopes of work and skillsets. Let's compare some of the key differences:

Programming Languages

Front-end languages: HTML, CSS, JavaScript, TypeScript

Back-end languages: Java, Python, Ruby, C#, PHP, Node.js

Front-end developers write code using HTML, CSS and JavaScript that runs on the client browser. Back-end developers write server-side code in languages like Java, C# that powers the application logic.

Code Execution Environment

Front-end code runs on the client, like the browser.

Back-end code runs on the server.

For example, React code is executed by the browser after it is delivered to the client. In contrast, Ruby on Rails code runs on the application server like Puma or Unicorn.

Data Interaction

Front-end uses APIs to fetch, mutate data.

Back-end provides APIs for CRUD data operations.

For example, a React front-end would use Axios to invoke REST APIs exposed by a Django back-end to load or update data in the Postgres database.

User Interface

Front-end is focused on UI/UX design.

Back-end has no user interface.

Front-end engineers work on crafting intuitive, appealing visual interfaces. Back-end engineers work on APIs, services, databases without UI concerns.

Security

Front-end has minimal security logic.

Back-end handles authentication, authorization, encryption.

For example, the back-end generates JWT tokens on successful user logins which are stored client-side and sent on subsequent requests.

Performance Optimization

Front-end uses caching, CDNs to optimize performance.

Back-end handles database optimization, infrastructure scaling.

Front-end can leverage browser caching, content delivery networks to improve performance. Back-end can scale databases, use object caching, fine tune queries etc.

Complexity

Front-end business logic is relatively simple.

Back-end handles complex business logic.

Validating form fields, showing notifications are simpler examples of front-end logic. Payment processing, data analytics are complex back-end logic.

In summary, front-end and back-end development require very distinct skillsets even though they work closely together. Specializing in either allows developers to go really deep into particular technology stacks and workflows.

1.4 Overview of popular back-end languages and frameworks

There are many technology options available for developing robust and scalable backend applications. Some of the most widely used languages and frameworks include:

Python + Django

Python is an interpreted, high-level programming language. It emphasizes code readability and rapid prototyping. Some key advantages of Python for backend development are:

- Large standard library with batteries-included modules for various tasks

- Dynamic typing allows faster development iterations

- Easy to read and maintainable code

- Mature package ecosystem and open source libraries

Django is a popular Python web framework based on the model-template-views architectural pattern. Key features:

- Object-relational mapper (ORM) for working with databases

- Modular design promotes code reusability

- Admin interface generation to manage database content

- Built-in security protections against attacks like SQL injections, cross-site scripting etc.

Sample Django code to retrieve articles from database:

```python
from .models import Article


def list_articles():
    articles = Article.objects.all()
    return render(request, 'articles.html', {'articles': articles})
```

Ruby on Rails

Ruby is an open source dynamic programming language optimized for developer productivity and enjoyable coding experience. Rails is a MVC framework for building web apps in Ruby. Notable features:

- Convention over configuration philosophy reduces boilerplate code

- ActiveRecord ORM provides database access

- Migrations help evolve database schema alongside code changes

- Robust ecosystem of third-party gems (libraries)

Sample Rails code for a RESTful Articles controller:

```ruby
class ArticlesController < ApplicationController

  # GET /articles
```

```
  def index
    @articles = Article.all
  end


  # GET /articles/:id
  def show
    @article = Article.find(params[:id])
  end


  # POST /articles
  def create
    # Save new article
  end


end
```


Java + Spring

Java is a statically typed, object-oriented language optimized for robustness and performance. Spring Framework is an application framework and inversion of control container for Java.

Advantages:

- Statically typed, fast execution

- Spring's dependency injection promotes loose coupling

- Spring MVC follows model-view-controller architecture

- Easy integration with Java EE and other Jakarta EE technologies

Sample Spring MVC controller:

```java
@Controller
public class ArticleController {

  @Autowired
  private ArticleService articleService;

  @GetMapping("/articles")
  public String listArticles(Model model) {
    model.addAttribute("articles", articleService.listArticles());
    return "articles";
  }

}
```

Other popular options include ASP.NET, Node.js, Laravel, Express.js etc. The right technology depends on application requirements, existing infrastructure, team skills and other constraints.

CHAPTER II
Setting up back-end development environment

2.1 Installing languages and frameworks

Choosing the right code editor is a crucial decision for any developer. It's the tool where you'll spend

Here are some tips on installing languages and frameworks for back-end development:

Setting up a development environment is the first step towards building a new back-end application. Here are some guidelines on installing languages and frameworks:

Installing Python

Python runs on Windows, MacOS and Linux operating systems. To install:

- On Windows, download the installer from python.org and run it. Tick the "Add Python to PATH" option during installation.

- On Mac, use Homebrew - `brew install python`. This also installs pip for managing packages.

- On Linux, use the system package manager like apt on Ubuntu - `sudo apt install python`.

After installing, verify with `python --version`.

It is also recommended to create isolated environments using virtualenv or poetry for each Python project, to manage dependencies properly.

Installing Node.js and npm

Download the LTS installer from nodejs.org and run it. This installs both Node.js and npm (Node Package Manager).

Or use nvm (Node Version Manager) to switch between Node versions:

```
nvm install node # Install latest version
nvm use node # Use latest version
```

Check the installation with `node -v` and `npm -v`.

Installing Ruby and Rails

For Ruby:

- On Windows, use the RubyInstaller

- On Mac, use Homebrew - `brew install ruby`

- On Linux, use `apt install ruby-full`

For Rails, use the gem package manager:

```
gem install rails
```

Installing Java and Spring Boot

Use SDKMAN to easily switch between Java versions:

```
sdk install java 8.0.282-zulu
sdk use java 8.0.282-zulu
```

Install Spring Boot CLI:

```
sdk install springboot
spring --version
```

Installing Databases

Some popular relational and NoSQL databases include:

- MySQL: Download mysql installer for Windows or use Homebrew on Mac.

- MongoDB: `brew install mongodb` on Mac or `apt install mongodb` on Ubuntu.

- PostgreSQL: Download installer from postgres site or use Homebrew on Mac.

Proper environment setup is key for smooth back-end development. Use virtual environments, containers like Docker to avoid version conflicts between projects.

2.2 Setting up IDEs and code editors

An IDE (Integrated Development Environment) or code editor is an essential tool for efficiently writing, navigating and understanding back-end code. Here are some popular options:

Visual Studio Code

VS Code is a lightweight yet powerful open-source code editor supporting a wide variety of languages and frameworks.

To get started:

- Download and install VS Code for your OS

- Install relevant extensions like Python, Django, Java, Spring Boot, Node.js etc.

- Enable syntax highlighting, code completion, linting for supported languages

- Integrate terminal within VS Code

PyCharm

PyCharm is an IDE specifically tailored for Python development. Key features:

- Integration with major Python frameworks like Django, Flask, Pandas, Jupyter

- Database tools and SQL editor

- Debugger, code inspections, refactors

- VCS support, remote development capabilities

To set up:

- Download and install PyCharm Community or Professional edition

- Configure Python interpreter and create project

- Install packages, set up virtual environment

- Enable Django support if using Django

IntelliJ IDEA

IntelliJ IDEA is a Java IDE with full-stack development capabilities. Steps to configure:

- Download and install IntelliJ IDEA

- Select project SDK (JDK) during project setup

- Enable frameworks like Spring, Micronaut, Jakarta EE

- Integrate build tools like Maven and Gradle

- Install Java, web development plugins as needed

Visual Studio

Visual Studio is Microsoft's IDE for languages like C#, ASP.NET, .NET Core. notable features:

- IntelliSense for smart code completion

- Built-in debugger

- Integration with SQL Server

- Cloud development with Azure

- Cross-platform development support

Atom, Sublime Text are other lightweight text editor alternatives. Choose an IDE or editor aligned with specific back-end stack requirements for maximum productivity.

2.3 Understanding back-end project structure

Back-end projects organized in a standardized structure help separate concerns and make code maintainable as the app grows. Here are some key folders and files:

/src

Contains the source code organized into subdirectories like:

/controllers - Handles incoming HTTP requests and routing

/services - Business logic layer, processes data and coordinates workflows

/models - Classes representing database models and entities

/utils - Common utility functions

/config - Environment-specific configuration

/tests - Test cases for code

/routes.js - Maps endpoints to controller actions

/server.js - Entry point that boots up server, middleware, starts listening on port

/app.js - Initializes application, sets up middleware

/package.json - Lists third party packages/dependencies

Common patterns like MVC (Model View Controller) and MVVM (Model View ViewModel) also influence project structure.

A sample MVC project structure would be:

```
- app.js

- package.json

- controllers/

  - articleController.js

  - userController.js

- models/

  - Article.js

  - User.js

- views/

  - articles/

    - index.html

    - show.html
```

```
  - users/
    - index.html

- routes.js
```

The src is further organized into production code vs configurable code:

/src/main - Application sources

/src/test - Test code

Other common top-level folders:

/docs - Documentation

/scripts - Build and deployment bash/shell scripts

- /dist or /build - Packaged artifacts for deployment

Having a consistent project structure makes back-end code predictable and maintainable as the project scales up.

2.4 Working with version control systems like Git

Version control systems like Git are essential for tracking code changes and enabling collaboration in back-end projects. Here is a typical Git workflow:

Install Git

- On Mac or Linux, Git comes pre-installed

- On Windows, download and install Git bash

Initialize Repo

- `git init` initializes a new Git repo in the project folder

- This creates a hidden .git subdirectory

Make Commits

- `git add <files>` stages files for commit

- `git commit -m "message"` commits staged snapshots

- Commit related changes in small commits with descriptive messages

Manage Branches

- `git branch` shows branches

- `git branch <name>` creates a new branch

- `git switch <branch>` switches to branch

- Use separate branches for features or fixes

Merge and Rebase

- `git merge <branch>` merges branch into current branch

- `git rebase <branch>` reapplies commits on top of branch

- Rebase to avoid messy merge commits, keep history linear

Remotes and Pushing Code

- `git remote add origin <url>` adds remote origin

- `git push -u origin main` pushes commits to default remote

- `git pull` fetches updates from remote repo

- Push to and pull from remotes like GitHub to share code

Version tagging

- `git tag v1.0.0` tags release points like versions

- `git push --tags` pushes tags to remote repo

- Tagging allows identifying release points across branches

Git enables distributed collaboration, branching, merging workflows essential for large back-end teams.

2.5 Install packages using npm, yarn, etc.

Modern backend development relies heavily on third-party packages for faster and better software delivery. Package managers streamline installing, upgrading and removing external dependencies.

npm for Node.js

npm is the default package manager for Node.js. To use npm:

- Initialize npm in a project folder with `npm init`

- This creates a package.json manifest file

- Install a package like Express.js web framework

  `npm install express`

- Specify version numbers to install an exact version

  `npm install express@4.17.1`

- Save packages to package.json during install

  `npm install express --save`

- Install all dependencies from package.json

  `npm install`

- Uninstall packages

  `npm uninstall express`

- Update packages

  `npm update` checks for updates
  `npm update express` updates just Express

- Search npm registry for packages

  `npm search <query>`

- Create an immutable lockfile called package-lock.json

  `npm install --package-lock`

npm is configurable using a .npmrc file. Useful for setting registry URLs, cache locations etc.

Yarn for Node.js

Yarn is an alternative package manager for Node focused on speed and security.

- Install Yarn using `npm install -g yarn`

- Initialize Yarn using `yarn init`

- Install packages using `yarn add express`

- Upgrade, remove, list packages using `yarn up`, `yarn remove`, `yarn list`

- Yarn creates a yarn.lock lockfile by default

Compared to npm, Yarn is faster, uses lockfiles by default, and has a more secure install process.

Pip for Python

Pip is the standard package manager for Python. Usage:

- Install packages using `pip install django`

- Specify versions like `pip install django==2.2.6`

- Upgrade pip packages using `pip install --upgrade django`

- Uninstall using `pip uninstall django`

- Search PyPI registry `pip search query`

- Manage packages in a virtual environment to avoid conflicts

- Requirements.txt lists production packages

Poetry, Pipenv are other Python package managers gaining popularity.

In summary, backend developers should leverage package managers like npm, Yarn and Pip to efficiently reuse third-party open source libraries and frameworks.

CHAPTER III
Back-end programming fundamentals

3.1 Syntax, variables, data types in Python, Java, C#, PHP, etc.

In this chapter, we'll delve into the fundamental concepts of back-end programming. We'll explore the syntax, variables, and data types in popular programming languages like Python, Java, C#, PHP, and more. This foundation is crucial for understanding and building robust back-end applications.

3.1 Syntax, Variables, and Data Types

Syntax Overview

Syntax refers to the set of rules that dictate how programs written in a particular language should be structured. It encompasses elements such as variable naming conventions, statement terminators, and indentation. Let's examine the syntax basics in a few programming languages:

Python:

```python
# Python uses indentation to denote code blocks
if True:
```

```
    print("Hello, World!")

# Variables are dynamically typed
x = 5  # Integer
y = "Hello"  # String
```

Java:
```java
// Java uses semicolons to terminate statements
if (true) {
    System.out.println("Hello, World!");
}

// Variables must be explicitly typed
int x = 5;  // Integer
String y = "Hello";  // String
```

C#:
```csharp
// C# uses semicolons to terminate statements
if (true) {
    Console.WriteLine("Hello, World!");
}
```

// Variables must be explicitly typed

int x = 5; // Integer

string y = "Hello"; // String

```

**PHP:**

```php
// PHP uses semicolons to terminate statements
if (true) {
    echo "Hello, World!";
}

// Variables start with a dollar sign and are loosely typed
$x = 5;  // Integer
$y = "Hello";  // String
```

Data Types

Each programming language supports various data types to represent different kinds of values. Common data types include integers, floating-point numbers, strings, and booleans.

Python:

```python
```
```

```python
# Common data types in Python
x = 5  # Integer
y = 3.14  # Float
z = "Hello"  # String
is_valid = True  # Boolean
```

Java:
```java
// Common data types in Java
int x = 5;  // Integer
double y = 3.14;  // Double
String z = "Hello";  // String
boolean is_valid = true;  // Boolean
```

C#:
```csharp
// Common data types in C#
int x = 5;  // Integer
double y = 3.14;  // Double
string z = "Hello";  // String
bool is_valid = true;  // Boolean
```

PHP:

```php
// Common data types in PHP
$x = 5;  // Integer
$y = 3.14;  // Float
$z = "Hello";  // String
$is_valid = true; // Boolean
```

Understanding syntax, variables, and data types is the foundation for writing code in any programming language. As you progress in back-end development, these concepts will become second nature, enabling you to build robust and efficient applications.

3.2 Control flows, loops, conditional statements

Control flows, loops, and conditional statements are essential constructs in programming that allow you to control the flow of your code. In this section, we'll explore these concepts in detail using examples in Python, Java, C#, and PHP.

3.2.1 Conditional Statements

Conditional statements enable you to make decisions in your code based on certain conditions. The most common conditional statements are `if`, `else if` (or `elif` in Python), and `else`.

Python:

```python
age = 25
if age < 18:
    print("You are a minor.")
elif age >= 18 and age < 65:
    print("You are an adult.")
else:
    print("You are a senior citizen.")
```

Java:

```java
int age = 25;
if (age < 18) {
```

        System.out.println("You are a minor.");

} else if (age >= 18 && age < 65) {

        System.out.println("You are an adult.");

} else {

        System.out.println("You are a senior citizen.");

}
```


**C#:**

```csharp
int age = 25;

if (age < 18) {

        Console.WriteLine("You are a minor.");

} else if (age >= 18 && age < 65) {

        Console.WriteLine("You are an adult.");

} else {

        Console.WriteLine("You are a senior citizen.");

}
```


PHP:

```php
$age = 25;

if ($age < 18) {

        echo "You are a minor.";
```
```

```
} elseif ($age >= 18 && $age < 65) {

   echo "You are an adult.";

} else {

   echo "You are a senior citizen.";

}
```

3.2.2 Loops

Loops are used for repetitive tasks, allowing you to execute a block of code multiple times. Common loop types include `for`, `while`, and `do-while`.

Python:

```python
# Using a for loop to iterate over a list
fruits = ["apple", "banana", "cherry"]
for fruit in fruits:
    print(fruit)
```

Java:

```java
// Using a for loop to iterate over an array
String[] fruits = {"apple", "banana", "cherry"};
for (String fruit : fruits) {
```

```
    System.out.println(fruit);
}
```


C#:

```csharp
// Using a for loop to iterate over an array
string[] fruits = { "apple", "banana", "cherry" };
foreach (string fruit in fruits) {
    Console.WriteLine(fruit);
}
```


PHP:

```php
// Using a foreach loop to iterate over an array
$fruits = ["apple", "banana", "cherry"];
foreach ($fruits as $fruit) {
    echo $fruit . "\n";
}
```


3.2.3 Control Flow

Control flow statements, such as `break` and `continue`, allow you to alter the flow of execution within loops or switch between different branches of conditional statements.

Python:

```python
# Using break to exit a loop prematurely
for i in range(5):
    if i == 3:
        break
    print(i)  # Prints 0, 1, 2
```

Java:

```java
// Using break to exit a loop prematurely
for (int i = 0; i < 5; i++) {
    if (i == 3) {
        break;
    }
    System.out.println(i);  // Prints 0, 1, 2
}
```

C#:

```csharp
```

```
// Using break to exit a loop prematurely
for (int i = 0; i < 5; i++) {
    if (i == 3) {
        break;
    }
    Console.WriteLine(i);  // Prints 0, 1, 2
}
```

PHP:

```php
// Using break to exit a loop prematurely
for ($i = 0; $i < 5; $i++) {
    if ($i == 3) {
        break;
    }
    echo $i . "\n";  // Prints 0, 1, 2
}
```

Understanding control flows, loops, and conditional statements is vital for building decision-making logic and iterating through data in your back-end applications. These constructs provide the foundation for more complex programming tasks as you advance in back-end development.

3.3 Functions, classes, objects, inheritance

In this section, we will explore the fundamental concepts of functions, classes, objects, and inheritance in programming languages like Python, Java, C#, and PHP. These concepts form the building blocks of object-oriented programming (OOP) and are crucial for creating organized, reusable, and efficient code.

3.3.1 Functions

Functions are blocks of code that perform a specific task. They take input (parameters) and can return output. Functions promote code modularity and reusability.

Python:

```python
# Defining a simple function
def greet(name):
    return "Hello, " + name + "!"


# Calling the function
message = greet("Alice")
print(message)  # Output: Hello, Alice!
```

Java:

```java
// Defining a simple function
```

```java
public String greet(String name) {

    return "Hello, " + name + "!";

}


// Calling the function

String message = greet("Alice");

System.out.println(message);  // Output: Hello, Alice!
```


C#:

```csharp
// Defining a simple function

public string Greet(string name) {

    return "Hello, " + name + "!";

}


// Calling the function

string message = Greet("Alice");

Console.WriteLine(message);  // Output: Hello, Alice!
```


PHP:

```php
// Defining a simple function

function greet($name) {
```

```php
    return "Hello, " . $name . "!";
}

// Calling the function
$message = greet("Alice");
echo $message;  // Output: Hello, Alice!
```

3.3.2 Classes and Objects

Classes are blueprints for creating objects. An object is an instance of a class. They encapsulate data (attributes) and behavior (methods) into a single entity.

Python:
```python
# Defining a class
class Person:
    def __init__(self, name, age):
        self.name = name
        self.age = age

    def greet(self):
        return f"Hello, my name is {self.name} and I am {self.age} years old."

# Creating an object
```

```python
alice = Person("Alice", 30)

# Accessing object attributes and calling methods
print(alice.name)    # Output: Alice
print(alice.greet()) # Output: Hello, my name is Alice and I am 30 years old.
```

Java:
```java
// Defining a class
public class Person {
    private String name;
    private int age;

    public Person(String name, int age) {
        this.name = name;
        this.age = age;
    }

    public String greet() {
        return "Hello, my name is " + name + " and I am " + age + " years old.";
    }
}

// Creating an object
```

```java
Person alice = new Person("Alice", 30);

// Accessing object attributes and calling methods
System.out.println(alice.getName());    // Output: Alice
System.out.println(alice.greet());       // Output: Hello, my name is Alice and I am 30 years old.
```

C#:

```csharp
// Defining a class
public class Person {
    public string Name { get; set; }
    public int Age { get; set; }

    public Person(string name, int age) {
        Name = name;
        Age = age;
    }

    public string Greet() {
        return "Hello, my name is " + Name + " and I am " + Age + " years old.";
    }
}

// Creating an object
```

```csharp
Person alice = new Person("Alice", 30);

// Accessing object attributes and calling methods
Console.WriteLine(alice.Name);        // Output: Alice
Console.WriteLine(alice.Greet());     // Output: Hello, my name is Alice and I am 30 years old.
```

PHP:

```php
// Defining a class
class Person {
    public $name;
    public $age;

    public function __construct($name, $age) {
        $this->name = $name;
        $this->age = $age;
    }

    public function greet() {
        return "Hello, my name is {$this->name} and I am {$this->age} years old.";
    }
}

// Creating an object
```

```php
$alice = new Person("Alice", 30);

// Accessing object attributes and calling methods
echo $alice->name;          // Output: Alice
echo $alice->greet();       // Output: Hello, my name is Alice and I am 30 years old.
```

3.3.3 Inheritance

Inheritance allows you to create a new class that inherits properties and methods from an existing class. It promotes code reuse and hierarchy in your codebase.

Python:

```python
# Defining a parent class
class Animal:
    def __init__(self, name):
        self.name = name

    def speak(self):
        pass  # To be overridden in child classes

# Defining child classes
class Dog(Animal):
    def speak(self):
```

```python
        return f"{self.name} says Woof!"

class Cat(Animal):
    def speak(self):
        return f"{self.name} says Meow!"

# Creating objects and invoking methods
dog = Dog("Buddy")
cat = Cat("Whiskers")
print(dog.speak())  # Output: Buddy says Woof!
print(cat.speak())  # Output: Whiskers says Meow!
```

Java, C#, and PHP follow similar principles of inheritance as Python.

Understanding functions, classes, objects, and inheritance is essential for creating well-structured and maintainable back-end code. These concepts enable you to organize your code logically and efficiently, making it easier to manage and extend your back-end applications.

3.4 Handling exceptions and errors

In this section, we'll dive into the crucial topic of handling exceptions and errors in programming. Properly managing exceptions is essential for writing robust and error-tolerant back-end code. We'll explore how to catch, handle, and raise exceptions using examples in Python, Java, C#, and PHP.

3.4.1 Understanding Exceptions

An exception is an unexpected or exceptional event that disrupts the normal flow of a program. It can occur for various reasons, such as invalid user input, file not found, or division by zero. Handling exceptions ensures that your program gracefully responds to errors instead of crashing.

3.4.2 Try-Catch Blocks

Try-catch blocks are used to catch and handle exceptions. Code inside the `try` block is executed, and if an exception occurs, it is caught in the corresponding `catch` block.

Python:

```python
try:
    result = 10 / 0  # This will raise a ZeroDivisionError
except ZeroDivisionError as e:
    print(f"Error: {e}")
```

Java:

```java
try {

    int result = 10 / 0;  // This will throw an ArithmeticException

} catch (ArithmeticException e) {

    System.out.println("Error: " + e.getMessage());

}
```


C#:

```csharp
try {

    int result = 10 / 0;  // This will throw a DivideByZeroException

} catch (DivideByZeroException e) {

    Console.WriteLine("Error: " + e.Message);

}
```


PHP:

```php
try {

    $result = 10 / 0;  // This will result in a DivisionByZeroError

} catch (DivisionByZeroError $e) {

    echo "Error: " . $e->getMessage();

}
```

3.4.3 Handling Multiple Exceptions

You can handle multiple exceptions by adding multiple `catch` blocks for different exception types.

Java:

```java
try {
    // Code that may throw exceptions
} catch (ArithmeticException e) {
    // Handle arithmetic exception
} catch (IOException e) {
    // Handle IO exception
} catch (Exception e) {
    // Handle other exceptions
}
```

3.4.4 The Finally Block

The `finally` block is used to specify code that must be executed regardless of whether an exception occurred or not.

Java:

```java
try {
    // Code that may throw exceptions
} catch (Exception e) {
    // Handle exception
} finally {
    // Cleanup code (e.g., closing resources)
}
```

3.4.5 Raising Custom Exceptions

You can create custom exceptions to handle application-specific errors.

Python:
```python
class CustomError(Exception):
    def __init__(self, message):
        super().__init__(message)

try:
    raise CustomError("This is a custom exception")
except CustomError as e:
    print(f"Custom Error: {e}")
```

Java:

```java
class CustomException extends Exception {

    public CustomException(String message) {

        super(message);

    }

}


try {

    throw new CustomException("This is a custom exception");

} catch (CustomException e) {

    System.out.println("Custom Error: " + e.getMessage());

}
```


C#:

```csharp
class CustomException : Exception {

    public CustomException(string message) : base(message) {

    }

}


try {

    throw new CustomException("This is a custom exception");
```

```
} catch (CustomException e) {
    Console.WriteLine("Custom Error: " + e.Message);
}
```

PHP:

```php
class CustomException extends Exception {}

try {
    throw new CustomException("This is a custom exception");
} catch (CustomException $e) {
    echo "Custom Error: " . $e->getMessage();
}
```

3.4.6 Best Practices

- Catch exceptions at the appropriate level in your code.
- Provide meaningful error messages for exceptions.
- Use custom exceptions for application-specific errors.
- Clean up resources (e.g., file handles, database connections) in the `finally` block.
- Handle exceptions gracefully to prevent program crashes.

Understanding how to handle exceptions and errors is crucial for building reliable back-end applications. It ensures that your code can gracefully recover from unexpected situations and provides a better experience for users.

3.5 Automated testing basics

In this section, we will explore the fundamentals of automated testing, an essential practice in software development that ensures the reliability and correctness of your back-end applications. We will discuss different types of tests, testing frameworks, and provide examples in Python, Java, C#, and PHP.

3.5.1 Why Automated Testing?

Automated testing helps in:

- Detecting and preventing regressions (unexpected bugs introduced by code changes).

- Ensuring that new features do not break existing functionality.

- Providing documentation for how your code is supposed to work.

- Facilitating collaborative development by allowing multiple team members to validate code changes.

3.5.2 Types of Automated Tests

1. Unit Tests: These tests focus on testing individual components or functions in isolation. They ensure that each piece of your code behaves correctly.

2. Integration Tests: Integration tests verify that different components of your application work together as expected. They test the interactions between modules, classes, or services.

3. Functional Tests: Functional tests examine your application from a high-level perspective. They validate that the entire application or specific features function correctly.

4. End-to-End (E2E) Tests: E2E tests simulate real user interactions with your application, from start to finish. They verify that your application works as expected from a user's perspective.

3.5.3 Testing Frameworks

Different programming languages have various testing frameworks to facilitate automated testing. Let's explore examples in Python, Java, C#, and PHP.

Python (using `unittest`):

```python
import unittest

def add(a, b):
    return a + b

class TestAddition(unittest.TestCase):
    def test_add_positive_numbers(self):
        result = add(3, 4)
        self.assertEqual(result, 7)

    def test_add_negative_numbers(self):
        result = add(-2, -5)
        self.assertEqual(result, -7)
```

```
if __name__ == "__main__":
    unittest.main()
```


Java (using JUnit):

```java
import org.junit.jupiter.api.Test;
import static org.junit.jupiter.api.Assertions.*;

public class CalculatorTest {
    @Test
    void testAddition() {
        assertEquals(7, Calculator.add(3, 4));
    }

    @Test
    void testSubtraction() {
        assertEquals(1, Calculator.subtract(5, 4));
    }
}
```


C# (using NUnit):

```csharp
using NUnit.Framework;
```

```csharp
public class CalculatorTests {

    [Test]

    public void TestAddition() {

        Assert.AreEqual(7, Calculator.Add(3, 4));

    }


    [Test]

    public void TestSubtraction() {

        Assert.AreEqual(1, Calculator.Subtract(5, 4));

    }

}
```


PHP (using PHPUnit):

```php
use PHPUnit\Framework\TestCase;

class CalculatorTest extends TestCase {

    public function testAddition() {

        $this->assertEquals(7, Calculator::add(3, 4));

    }


    public function testSubtraction() {

        $this->assertEquals(1, Calculator::subtract(5, 4));
```

```
    }
  }
```

3.5.4 Running Tests

You can run tests using the testing framework's command-line interface or integrated development environment (IDE) tools.

- Python: `python -m unittest test_module`

- Java: Use your IDE's JUnit runner or `mvn test` (Maven) or `gradle test` (Gradle).

- C#: Use the Visual Studio Test Explorer or run `dotnet test`.

- PHP: `phpunit test_file`

3.5.5 Continuous Integration (CI)

Automated tests are often integrated into a CI/CD (Continuous Integration/Continuous Deployment) pipeline. CI tools like Jenkins, Travis CI, CircleCI, and GitHub Actions automatically run tests whenever code changes are pushed, ensuring that your application remains reliable.

Automated testing is a critical aspect of software development, helping you catch and fix bugs early in the development process. It promotes code quality and confidence in your back-end applications, making them more robust and maintainable.

CHAPTER IV
Building REST APIs

4.1 Overview of REST architecture

REST (Representational State Transfer) is an architectural style for designing networked applications. It is based on a set of principles that promote scalability, simplicity, and uniformity in how data is requested and manipulated over the web. In this section, we will provide a detailed overview of REST architecture, including its key concepts and principles.

4.1.1 Key Concepts of REST

1. Resources: In REST, everything is a resource. A resource can be a physical object (e.g., a book), a digital concept (e.g., an image), or any other entity that can be identified using a URL (Uniform Resource Locator).

2. HTTP Methods: REST uses HTTP methods (GET, POST, PUT, DELETE, etc.) to perform CRUD (Create, Read, Update, Delete) operations on resources. Each HTTP method has a specific meaning:

- GET: Retrieve data from a resource.

- POST: Create a new resource.

- PUT: Update an existing resource or create a new one if it doesn't exist.

- DELETE: Remove a resource.

- And others like PATCH, HEAD, and OPTIONS.

3. Statelessness: REST is stateless, meaning that each request from a client to a server must contain all the information needed to understand and process the request. There should be no server-side session or state stored between requests.

4. Uniform Interface: REST defines a uniform and consistent interface between clients and servers. This simplifies the architecture and allows components to evolve independently.

4.1.2 Resources and URLs

Resources are identified using URLs, and the structure of URLs in RESTful APIs is hierarchical and meaningful. For example:

- `https://api.example.com/books`: Represents a collection of books.

- `https://api.example.com/books/123`: Represents a specific book with the ID 123.

4.1.3 Representations

Resources can have multiple representations, such as JSON, XML, HTML, or even images. Clients can specify their preferred representation format using HTTP headers.

4.1.4 Statelessness

As mentioned earlier, REST is stateless. Each request from a client to a server should contain all the necessary information, and the server should not store any client-specific data between requests. This enables easy scalability and fault tolerance.

4.1.5 CRUD Operations

RESTful APIs typically map CRUD operations to HTTP methods as follows:

- `GET`: Retrieve data (Read).

- `POST`: Create new data (Create).

- `PUT` or `PATCH`: Update data (Update).

- `DELETE`: Remove data (Delete).

4.1.6 Example Request-Response Cycle

Let's illustrate a simple example of a RESTful request-response cycle using Python and the `requests` library.

```python
import requests

# Making a GET request to retrieve a resource
response = requests.get("https://api.example.com/books/123")

# Checking the response status code
if response.status_code == 200:
    book_data = response.json()  # Parsing JSON response
    print("Book Title:", book_data["title"])
else:
    print("Failed to retrieve the book.")
```

```

In this example:

- We make a GET request to retrieve a specific book resource using its URL.

- We check the HTTP status code (200 means success).

- If successful, we parse the JSON response and extract the book title.


This is a basic overview of REST architecture, highlighting its key principles and concepts. In the subsequent sections of this chapter, we will delve deeper into API design, CRUD operations, request and response handling, versioning, documentation, and testing of REST APIs, building upon this foundational knowledge.
```

4.2 API design principles and best practices

Designing a well-structured and user-friendly API is crucial for the success of any RESTful service. In this section, we will explore the key API design principles and best practices to help you create robust, maintainable, and developer-friendly APIs.

Understand Your Users

Before designing an API, it's essential to understand the needs and expectations of your API users (developers who will consume your API). Consider their use cases, the data they need, and the actions they want to perform. This user-centric approach ensures that your API provides value to its consumers.

Use Descriptive Resource URLs

Resource URLs should be descriptive and self-explanatory. They should clearly represent the resource being accessed or manipulated. For example:

- Good: `/books/123`

- Bad: `/fetchData`

A well-structured URL improves the readability of your API and helps developers understand its functionality.

HTTP Methods for CRUD Operations

Use HTTP methods as per their intended purpose for CRUD (Create, Read, Update, Delete) operations:

- `GET` for retrieval of data.

- `POST` for creating new resources.

- `PUT` or `PATCH` for updating existing resources.

- `DELETE` for removing resources.

Use HTTP Status Codes

HTTP status codes convey the outcome of an API request. Use appropriate status codes to indicate the result of each operation:

- `200 OK` for successful responses.

- `201 Created` for successful resource creation.

- `204 No Content` for successful resource deletion.

- `400 Bad Request` for client-side errors (e.g., invalid input).

- `404 Not Found` for resources that don't exist.

- `500 Internal Server Error` for server-side errors.

Version Your API

API versions prevent breaking changes from affecting existing users. Include a version number in the API URL to maintain backward compatibility. For example:

- `https://api.example.com/v1/books`

- `https://api.example.com/v2/books`

Use Pagination and Filtering

When returning large datasets, implement pagination to limit the number of results per page. Allow clients to specify filters to narrow down results based on criteria. For example, use query parameters like `page`, `limit`, and `filter`.

Authentication and Authorization

Implement secure authentication and authorization mechanisms to protect your API. Common methods include API keys, OAuth2, and JWT (JSON Web Tokens). Ensure that users can only access resources they have permission to access.

Rate Limiting

Implement rate limiting to prevent abuse and ensure fair usage of your API. Specify the number of requests allowed per minute or hour for each user or API key.

Documentation

Comprehensive and up-to-date documentation is essential. Use tools like Swagger, OpenAPI, or Postman to generate API documentation. Include examples, request/response schemas, and usage guidelines to assist developers.

Version Control

Apply version control to your API design. Changes to the API should be documented, and new versions should be introduced gradually to minimize disruption for existing users.

Error Handling

Design informative and consistent error responses. Include error codes, descriptions, and suggestions for resolution. Make error responses machine-readable for ease of handling by client applications.

Testing

Thoroughly test your API, covering different scenarios, error cases, and edge cases. Automated testing ensures that changes do not introduce regressions.

Security

Implement security best practices, including data encryption, input validation, and protection against common web vulnerabilities like SQL injection and Cross-Site Scripting (XSS) attacks.

Rate Your API

Consider providing a usage dashboard or metrics for users to monitor their API usage. This transparency fosters trust and helps users understand their consumption patterns.

By adhering to these API design principles and best practices, you can create an API that is not only functional but also user-friendly, secure, and scalable. Effective API design is a critical factor in the success of your back-end service.

4.3 Implementing CRUD operations

In this section, we will dive into the practical implementation of CRUD (Create, Read, Update, Delete) operations in a RESTful API. We'll discuss how to create, retrieve, update, and delete resources using HTTP methods and provide examples in Python using the Flask framework.

4.3.1 Setting Up the Environment

Before implementing CRUD operations, ensure you have a development environment set up. You'll need Python and a web framework like Flask. Install Flask using `pip`:

```bash
pip install Flask
```

4.3.2 Creating Resources

To create resources, we use the HTTP `POST` method. Here's how you can create a new book resource:

```python
from flask import Flask, request, jsonify

app = Flask(__name__)

# Sample data (in-memory storage)
```

```python
books = []

@app.route('/books', methods=['POST'])
def create_book():
    data = request.get_json()
    if 'title' not in data or 'author' not in data:
        return jsonify({'error': 'Title and author are required'}), 400

    book = {
        'id': len(books) + 1,
        'title': data['title'],
        'author': data['author']
    }
    books.append(book)

    return jsonify({'message': 'Book created', 'book': book}), 201

if __name__ == '__main__':
    app.run(debug=True)
```

- We define a `/books` route that listens for `POST` requests.

- We extract the JSON data from the request body and validate that it contains the required fields (`title` and `author`).

- If the data is valid, we create a new book object, assign it a unique ID, and add it to our in-memory storage.

- We return a JSON response with a success message and the created book.

4.3.3 Retrieving Resources

To retrieve resources, we use the HTTP `GET` method. Here's how you can retrieve all books or a specific book by ID:

```python
@app.route('/books', methods=['GET'])
def get_books():
    return jsonify({'books': books})


@app.route('/books/<int:book_id>', methods=['GET'])
def get_book(book_id):
    book = next((b for b in books if b['id'] == book_id), None)
    if book is None:
        return jsonify({'error': 'Book not found'}), 404
    return jsonify({'book': book})
```

- The `/books` route listens for `GET` requests and returns a JSON response with all books.

- The `/books/<int:book_id>` route listens for `GET` requests with a specific book ID as a URL parameter. It retrieves the book with the matching ID or returns a 404 error if not found.

4.3.4 Updating Resources

To update resources, we use the HTTP `PUT` or `PATCH` method. Here's how you can update a book by ID:

```python
@app.route('/books/<int:book_id>', methods=['PUT'])
def update_book(book_id):
    book = next((b for b in books if b['id'] == book_id), None)
    if book is None:
        return jsonify({'error': 'Book not found'}), 404

    data = request.get_json()
    book['title'] = data.get('title', book['title'])
    book['author'] = data.get('author', book['author'])

    return jsonify({'message': 'Book updated', 'book': book})

# Alternatively, you can implement a PATCH request to update specific fields.
@app.route('/books/<int:book_id>', methods=['PATCH'])
def partial_update_book(book_id):
    book = next((b for b in books if b['id'] == book_id), None)
    if book is None:
        return jsonify({'error': 'Book not found'}), 404
```

```python
    data = request.get_json()

    if 'title' in data:
        book['title'] = data['title']

    if 'author' in data:
        book['author'] = data['author']


    return jsonify({'message': 'Book updated', 'book': book})
```

- The `/books/<int:book_id>` route with `PUT` updates the entire book resource. It retrieves the existing book, applies the changes from the request data, and returns the updated book.

- The `/books/<int:book_id>` route with `PATCH` allows partial updates. It updates only the fields provided in the request data.

4.3.5 Deleting Resources

To delete resources, we use the HTTP `DELETE` method. Here's how you can delete a book by ID:


```python
@app.route('/books/<int:book_id>', methods=['DELETE'])

def delete_book(book_id):

    book = next((b for b in books if b['id'] == book_id), None)

    if book is None:

        return jsonify({'error': 'Book not found'}), 404
```

```
    books.remove(book)

    return jsonify({'message': 'Book deleted', 'book': book})
```

- The `/books/<int:book_id>` route with `DELETE` finds the book with the specified ID and removes it from the collection.

Implementing CRUD operations is a fundamental aspect of building RESTful APIs. These operations allow clients to create, retrieve, update, and delete resources, providing a full range of functionality for your API users. The provided examples use Python and Flask, but the principles can be applied to other programming languages and frameworks.

4.4 Request and response handling

In this section, we will delve into the details of handling HTTP requests and responses within a RESTful API. Proper request handling and response formatting are crucial to building a robust and user-friendly API. We will provide examples in Python using the Flask framework to illustrate the concepts.

4.4.1 Setting Up the Environment

Before proceeding, make sure you have Flask installed, as mentioned in the previous sections.

4.4.2 Handling Requests

In a RESTful API, HTTP requests play a pivotal role. Here's how you can handle different types of requests:

1. Handling GET Requests:

```python
from flask import Flask, request, jsonify

app = Flask(__name__)

# Sample data (in-memory storage)
books = [...]
```

```python
@app.route('/books', methods=['GET'])
def get_books():
    # Retrieve all books
    return jsonify({'books': books})


@app.route('/books/<int:book_id>', methods=['GET'])
def get_book(book_id):
    # Retrieve a specific book by ID
    book = next((b for b in books if b['id'] == book_id), None)
    if book is None:
        return jsonify({'error': 'Book not found'}), 404
    return jsonify({'book': book})
```

- The `/books` route with `GET` retrieves a list of all books.
- The `/books/<int:book_id>` route with `GET` retrieves a specific book by its ID.

2. Handling POST Requests:

```python
@app.route('/books', methods=['POST'])
def create_book():
    data = request.get_json()
    # Validate and create a new book
    ...
```

```

- The `/books` route with `POST` creates a new book based on the data in the request body.

## 3. Handling PUT Requests:

```python
@app.route('/books/<int:book_id>', methods=['PUT'])
def update_book(book_id):
    # Update an existing book by ID
    data = request.get_json()
    ...
```

- The `/books/<int:book_id>` route with `PUT` updates an existing book using the provided data.

4. Handling DELETE Requests:

```python
@app.route('/books/<int:book_id>', methods=['DELETE'])
def delete_book(book_id):
    # Delete an existing book by ID
    ...
```
```

- The `/books/<int:book_id>` route with `DELETE` deletes a specific book by its ID.

4.4.3 Handling Responses

The format of responses is equally important for the usability of your API.

1. Formatting JSON Responses:

You can format responses as JSON objects using Flask's `jsonify` function:

```python
return jsonify({'key': 'value'})
```

2. Handling Status Codes:

HTTP status codes should reflect the outcome of the request. Use them accordingly:

- `200 OK` for successful responses.

- `201 Created` for resource creation.

- `204 No Content` for successful but empty responses.

- `400 Bad Request` for client errors.

- `404 Not Found` for resource not found.

- `500 Internal Server Error` for server errors.

3. Response Headers:

You can set custom response headers using Flask:

```python
response = jsonify({'key': 'value'})
response.headers['Custom-Header'] = 'Custom-Value'
return response
```

4. Customizing Response Data:

You can customize the response data based on your API's needs. For example, pagination or metadata can be added to responses to improve user experience.

```python
response_data = {
    'data': books,
    'page': 1,
    'total_pages': 3
}
return jsonify(response_data)
```

5. Error Handling:

For error responses, include informative error messages and status codes. Flask's `abort` function can be handy:

```python
from flask import abort

@app.route('/books/<int:book_id>', methods=['GET'])
def get_book(book_id):
    book = next((b for b in books if b['id'] == book_id), None)
    if book is None:
        abort(404, description="Book not found")
    return jsonify({'book': book})
```

Proper request and response handling is pivotal in building a user-friendly and reliable RESTful API. The provided examples demonstrate how to handle different types of HTTP requests and format responses using Flask, but the concepts can be applied to other web frameworks and programming languages as well.

4.5 Versioning, documentation and testing REST APIs

In this section, we will explore crucial aspects of building REST APIs: versioning, documentation, and testing. These practices are essential for maintaining a reliable and developer-friendly API.

4.5.1 Versioning Your API

API versioning allows you to introduce changes to your API without breaking existing clients. It ensures backward compatibility and a smooth transition for users when new features or modifications are introduced.

1. URL Versioning:

One common approach to versioning is to include the version number in the URL. For example:

- `https://api.example.com/v1/books`

- `https://api.example.com/v2/books`

2. Header Versioning:

Another approach is to specify the version in the request header. This can be done using a custom header like `Accept-Version`.

```http
GET /books HTTP/1.1
```

Host: api.example.com

Accept-Version: v1

```

Whichever method you choose, document the versioning strategy in your API documentation to inform users.

## 4.5.2 Documentation

Comprehensive and up-to-date documentation is critical for API adoption and ease of use. Effective documentation should provide clear guidance on how to use your API, including endpoints, request and response formats, authentication methods, and example use cases.

### 1. Use API Documentation Tools:

There are tools like Swagger, OpenAPI, and Postman that can help you generate interactive API documentation. These tools make it easier for developers to understand your API and test it.

### 2. Include Example Requests and Responses:

In your documentation, provide real-world examples of API requests and responses. This helps developers understand the expected data formats and usage.

### 3. Authentication and Authorization Details:
```

Explain how authentication and authorization work in your API. Provide examples of how to obtain and use API keys, OAuth tokens, or any other authentication mechanisms.

4. Rate Limiting and Usage Policies:

Clearly state your API's rate limiting policies and any usage restrictions. Inform developers of any limitations or quotas associated with their API usage.

5. Keep Documentation Updated:

As you make changes or updates to your API, remember to update your documentation accordingly. Outdated documentation can lead to confusion and errors.

4.5.3 Testing Your API

Testing is a critical part of API development. It ensures that your API works as expected and helps catch potential issues before they reach production.

1. Unit Testing:

Write unit tests for individual components of your API, such as controllers, services, and data models. Tools like `unittest` in Python or testing frameworks specific to your programming language can help.

2. Integration Testing:

Perform integration tests to ensure that different parts of your API work together correctly. This includes testing API endpoints, database interactions, and external service integrations.

3. Automated Testing:

Set up automated testing pipelines using tools like Jenkins, Travis CI, or GitHub Actions. Automate the execution of unit and integration tests whenever code changes are pushed.

4. Load Testing:

Conduct load testing to evaluate how your API performs under heavy traffic. Tools like Apache JMeter or locust.io can simulate a large number of concurrent users.

5. Security Testing:

Perform security testing to identify and mitigate vulnerabilities like SQL injection, XSS attacks, and unauthorized access. Tools like OWASP ZAP or Nessus can help with security scanning.

6. Documentation Testing:

Include tests for your API documentation. Ensure that examples, code snippets, and descriptions in your documentation accurately reflect the API's behavior.

By thoroughly testing your API, you can increase its reliability and stability, reduce the likelihood of bugs, and provide a better experience for users.

4.5.4 Continuous Integration and Delivery (CI/CD)

Integrate testing into your CI/CD pipeline to automate the process of building, testing, and deploying your API. CI/CD ensures that changes are tested and deployed quickly, helping you maintain a high level of code quality and reliability.

In summary, versioning, documentation, and testing are integral parts of building a successful and maintainable RESTful API. These practices not only ensure the reliability and usability of your API but also contribute to a positive developer experience.

CHAPTER V
Persisting Data in SQL Databases

5.1 Relational databases overview (MySQL, PostgreSQL, etc)

In this section, we will explore the fundamentals of relational databases, including popular options like MySQL, PostgreSQL, and others. We'll discuss the concepts, features, and basic operations associated with these databases.

5.1.1 What is a Relational Database?

A relational database is a structured way to store and manage data. It organizes data into tables with rows and columns, where each row represents a record, and each column represents a specific attribute or field of that record. The relational model uses relationships between tables to establish connections between data.

5.1.2 Popular Relational Database Management Systems (RDBMS)

There are several RDBMS options available, each with its unique features and use cases. Here are some of the most widely used ones:

MySQL: MySQL is known for its speed and scalability. It's often used in web applications and is open-source, making it a popular choice for small to medium-sized projects.

PostgreSQL: PostgreSQL is known for its advanced features, extensibility, and support for complex data types. It's a powerful open-source database suitable for various applications, including large-scale systems.

Oracle Database: Oracle Database is a commercial RDBMS known for its high performance, security, and reliability. It's commonly used in enterprise-level applications.

Microsoft SQL Server: SQL Server is a commercial RDBMS developed by Microsoft. It's known for its integration with Microsoft products and is often used in Windows-based environments.

SQLite: SQLite is a lightweight, embedded RDBMS that doesn't require a separate server process. It's suitable for mobile applications and small-scale projects.

5.1.3 Key Concepts in Relational Databases

Tables: Tables are the primary data structures in relational databases. Each table stores data related to a specific entity, such as customers, products, or orders.

Columns: Columns represent individual attributes of the data, such as names, dates, or quantities.

Rows: Rows, also known as records, represent individual instances of data within a table.

Primary Keys: Primary keys are unique identifiers for each row in a table. They ensure that each row can be uniquely identified.

Foreign Keys: Foreign keys establish relationships between tables. They are used to link rows in one table to rows in another, creating relationships like one-to-many or many-to-many.

SQL (Structured Query Language): SQL is the language used to interact with relational databases. It includes commands for creating, querying, updating, and deleting data.

5.1.4 Basic Operations in Relational Databases

Creating Tables:

To create a table in a relational database, you define its structure, including the columns and data types. Here's an example using SQL to create a "users" table:

```sql
CREATE TABLE users (
    id INT PRIMARY KEY,
    username VARCHAR(50),
    email VARCHAR(100),
    created_at TIMESTAMP
);
```

Inserting Data:

You can insert data into a table using SQL's `INSERT INTO` statement:

```sql
INSERT INTO users (id, username, email, created_at)
VALUES (1, 'john_doe', 'john@example.com', '2023-10-01 08:00:00');
```

Querying Data:

You can retrieve data from a table using SQL's `SELECT` statement:

```sql
SELECT * FROM users WHERE username = 'john_doe';
```

Updating Data:

To update existing data, use SQL's `UPDATE` statement:

```sql
UPDATE users SET email = 'new_email@example.com' WHERE id = 1;
```

Deleting Data:

To remove data, use SQL's `DELETE FROM` statement:

```sql
DELETE FROM users WHERE id = 1;
```

These are some of the foundational concepts and operations in relational databases. Understanding these principles is essential when working with SQL databases like MySQL, PostgreSQL, and others. In the next sections, we'll delve deeper into topics such as database schema design, SQL operations, and using Object-Relational Mapping (ORM) frameworks.

5.2 Database schema design

Database schema design is a critical step in building a relational database system. A well-designed schema ensures efficient data storage, retrieval, and maintenance. In this section, we'll explore the key principles and steps involved in creating a robust database schema.

5.2.1 Understanding the Requirements

Before designing a database schema, it's crucial to understand the requirements of your application. Gather information about the types of data you need to store, their relationships, and the expected volume of data. Consider the following aspects:

- **Entities:** Identify the main entities (e.g., users, products, orders) and their attributes (e.g., name, email, price).

- **Relationships:** Determine how entities are related to each other. For example, an order is related to a user, and a product can be part of multiple orders.

- **Data Integrity:** Define constraints and rules to maintain data integrity, such as unique keys, foreign keys, and validation rules.

- **Performance:** Consider performance requirements and optimize the schema for efficient data retrieval.

5.2.2 Entity-Relationship Diagram (ERD)

An Entity-Relationship Diagram (ERD) is a visual representation of the database schema's structure. It helps you visualize entities, their attributes, and the relationships between them.

Here's an example of an ERD for a simple e-commerce system:

```
```

User <---- Order ----> Product

+----+   +------+   +------+

| ID | | ID | | ID |

| | | User | | |

| | | Date | | Name |

| | | | | Price|

+----+   +------+   +------+

```
```

- Users can place orders, and each order belongs to a user.

- Orders can contain multiple products, and each product can appear in multiple orders.

5.2.3 Creating Tables

Once you have a clear understanding of your data model, you can start creating tables in your database. Each table corresponds to an entity in your ERD.

For example, to create a "Users" table in SQL:

```sql
CREATE TABLE Users (
    ID INT PRIMARY KEY,
    Username VARCHAR(50) NOT NULL,
    Email VARCHAR(100) UNIQUE,
    CreatedAt TIMESTAMP
);
```

- The `ID` column is the primary key.

- The `Username` column stores usernames.

- The `Email` column is unique to ensure email uniqueness.

- The `CreatedAt` column stores the creation timestamp.

Repeat this process for all other entities in your schema.

5.2.4 Defining Relationships

To represent relationships between entities, use foreign keys. For example, to link orders to users:

```sql
CREATE TABLE Orders (
```

ID INT PRIMARY KEY,

UserID INT,

OrderDate DATE,

FOREIGN KEY (UserID) REFERENCES Users(ID)

);

```

- The `UserID` column is a foreign key that references the `ID` column of the `Users` table.

## 5.2.5 Normalization

Normalization is the process of organizing data to minimize redundancy and dependency. It involves breaking down tables into smaller, related tables to reduce data duplication.

Common normal forms include 1NF (First Normal Form), 2NF, and 3NF. Ensuring your schema is at least in 3NF is a good practice for most applications.

## 5.2.6 Indexing

Create indexes on columns frequently used in queries to improve query performance. For example, to index the `Email` column in the `Users` table:

```sql
CREATE INDEX idx_email ON Users (Email);
```
```

Indexes speed up data retrieval but come with a storage cost, so use them judiciously.

5.2.7 Review and Optimization

Regularly review and optimize your database schema as your application evolves. Consider factors like query performance, data growth, and usage patterns.

In conclusion, designing a database schema requires careful planning and consideration of your application's requirements. By following these principles and best practices, you can create an efficient and well-structured database schema that meets your application's needs.

5.3 SQL data definition, manipulation and queries

In this section, we will delve into SQL (Structured Query Language) and explore the fundamental operations for defining database structures, manipulating data, and performing queries. SQL is the language used to interact with relational databases like MySQL, PostgreSQL, and others.

5.3.1 SQL Data Definition Language (DDL)

SQL's Data Definition Language (DDL) is used for defining and managing database structures. It includes operations such as creating tables, altering their structure, and deleting them.

1. Creating Tables:

To create a table, use the `CREATE TABLE` statement. Here's an example to create a "Users" table:

```sql
CREATE TABLE Users (
    ID INT PRIMARY KEY,
    Username VARCHAR(50) NOT NULL,
    Email VARCHAR(100) UNIQUE,
    CreatedAt TIMESTAMP
);
```

- `ID` is the primary key.

- `Username` and `Email` are columns with specific data types.

- `CreatedAt` is a timestamp column.

2. Modifying Tables:

You can alter existing tables using the `ALTER TABLE` statement. For example, to add a "LastName" column to the "Users" table:

```sql
ALTER TABLE Users
ADD LastName VARCHAR(50);
```

3. Deleting Tables:

To delete a table and its data, use the `DROP TABLE` statement:

```sql
DROP TABLE Users;
```

5.3.2 SQL Data Manipulation Language (DML)

SQL's Data Manipulation Language (DML) includes operations for adding, modifying, and deleting data in tables.

1. Inserting Data:

To insert data into a table, use the `INSERT INTO` statement. For example, to add a new user to the "Users" table:

```sql
INSERT INTO Users (ID, Username, Email, CreatedAt)
VALUES (1, 'john_doe', 'john@example.com', '2023-10-01 08:00:00');
```

2. Updating Data:

To update existing data, use the `UPDATE` statement. Here's how to change a user's email:

```sql
UPDATE Users
SET Email = 'new_email@example.com'
WHERE ID = 1;
```

3. Deleting Data:

To delete data, use the `DELETE FROM` statement. To remove a user:

```sql
DELETE FROM Users
WHERE ID = 1;
```

5.3.3 SQL Queries (SELECT)

SQL queries are used to retrieve data from tables. The most common SQL operation is the `SELECT` statement.

1. Basic SELECT:

To retrieve all columns from a table:

```sql
SELECT * FROM Users;
```

2. Filtering Rows:

To filter rows based on a condition:

```sql
SELECT * FROM Users
WHERE Email = 'john@example.com';
```

3. Sorting Rows:

To sort the result set:

```sql
SELECT * FROM Users
ORDER BY CreatedAt DESC;
```

4. Aggregating Data:

To perform aggregation functions like counting or summing:

```sql
SELECT COUNT(*) FROM Users;
```

5. Joining Tables:

To combine data from multiple tables:

```sql
SELECT Users.Username, Orders.OrderDate
FROM Users
JOIN Orders ON Users.ID = Orders.UserID;
```

5.3.4 SQL Joins

SQL joins are used to combine rows from two or more tables based on related columns. Common join types include INNER JOIN, LEFT JOIN, RIGHT JOIN, and FULL JOIN.

Here's an example of an INNER JOIN to retrieve users and their associated orders:

```sql
SELECT Users.Username, Orders.OrderDate
FROM Users
INNER JOIN Orders ON Users.ID = Orders.UserID;
```

5.3.5 SQL Indexing

Indexes improve query performance by allowing the database system to locate data quickly. To create an index on a column:

```sql
CREATE INDEX idx_email ON Users (Email);
```

Indexes should be used judiciously based on query patterns.

5.3.6 Transactions

SQL supports transactions to ensure data integrity. Use the `BEGIN`, `COMMIT`, and `ROLLBACK` statements to manage transactions.

```sql
BEGIN;
-- SQL statements
COMMIT;
-- or
ROLLBACK;
```

Transactions ensure that a series of operations either complete entirely or leave the database unchanged in case of failure.

In conclusion, SQL is a powerful language for defining, manipulating, and querying relational databases. Understanding the basics of DDL, DML, and SQL queries is essential for effective database management and application development.

5.4 Using ORM frameworks like Hibernate, Entity, etc.

Object-Relational Mapping (ORM) frameworks provide a higher-level abstraction for working with databases, allowing developers to interact with databases using object-oriented programming languages. In this section, we'll explore the use of ORM frameworks like Hibernate (for Java) and Entity Framework (for .NET) with practical examples.

5.4.1 What is ORM?

ORM frameworks bridge the gap between the relational database world and the object-oriented programming world. They allow you to define database tables and relationships as objects and perform database operations using familiar programming constructs.

Advantages of ORM:

- Eliminates the need to write raw SQL queries.

- Improves code maintainability by using native programming language constructs.

- Provides database independence, allowing you to switch between different database systems.

5.4.2 Using Hibernate (Java)

Step 1: Setting Up Hibernate

First, include the Hibernate library in your Java project. You can use a build tool like Maven or Gradle to manage dependencies.

```xml
<!-- Maven dependency for Hibernate -->
<dependency>
    <groupId>org.hibernate</groupId>
    <artifactId>hibernate-core</artifactId>
    <version>5.5.7.Final</version>
</dependency>
```

Step 2: Configuring Hibernate

Create a `hibernate.cfg.xml` file to configure Hibernate, specifying the database connection details and entity mappings. For example:

```xml
<hibernate-configuration>
  <session-factory>
    <!-- Database connection properties -->
    <property name="hibernate.connection.url">jdbc:mysql://localhost:3306/mydb</property>
    <property name="hibernate.connection.username">username</property>
    <property name="hibernate.connection.password">password</property>
```

```
<!-- Entity classes -->

<mapping class="com.example.User"/>

</session-factory>

</hibernate-configuration>
```

Step 3: Creating Entity Classes

Define Java classes representing database tables and annotate them with Hibernate annotations. For example, a `User` entity:

```java
@Entity
@Table(name = "users")
public class User {
    @Id
    @GeneratedValue(strategy = GenerationType.IDENTITY)
    private Long id;

    @Column(name = "username")
    private String username;

    @Column(name = "email")
    private String email;
```

```java
    // Getters and setters

}
```

Step 4: Using Hibernate in Code

Now, you can use Hibernate to perform database operations in your Java code:

```java
// Create a Hibernate SessionFactory

SessionFactory sessionFactory = new Configuration().configure().buildSessionFactory();


// Open a session

Session session = sessionFactory.openSession();


// Begin a transaction

Transaction transaction = session.beginTransaction();


// Perform database operations

User user = new User();

user.setUsername("john_doe");

user.setEmail("john@example.com");
```

```
session.save(user); // Insert a new user

User retrievedUser = session.get(User.class, 1L); // Retrieve a user by ID

// Commit the transaction
transaction.commit();

// Close the session and session factory
session.close();
sessionFactory.close();
```

5.4.3 Using Entity Framework (.NET)

Step 1: Setting Up Entity Framework

Entity Framework is typically available as part of the .NET ecosystem. Create a .NET project and add Entity Framework as a NuGet package.

Step 2: Creating Entity Classes

Define C# classes representing database tables. For example, a `User` entity:

```csharp
```

```csharp
public class User {

    public int ID { get; set; }

    public string Username { get; set; }

    public string Email { get; set; }

}
```

Step 3: Configuring DbContext

Create a DbContext class that represents your database context and includes DbSet properties for your entities.

```csharp
public class MyDbContext : DbContext {

    public DbSet<User> Users { get; set; }


    public MyDbContext(DbContextOptions<MyDbContext> options) : base(options) { }

}
```

Step 4: Using Entity Framework in Code

You can use Entity Framework to perform database operations in your .NET code:

```csharp
using (var context = new MyDbContext(options))
{
    // Insert a new user
    var user = new User { Username = "john_doe", Email = "john@example.com" };
    context.Users.Add(user);
    context.SaveChanges();

    // Retrieve a user by ID
    var retrievedUser = context.Users.Find(1);
}
```

ORM frameworks like Hibernate and Entity Framework simplify database interaction and help you focus on your application's business logic rather than low-level SQL queries. These frameworks are essential tools for modern application development.

5.5 Migration scripts and database optimization

In this section, we will explore the use of migration scripts and techniques for optimizing SQL databases to improve performance and maintainability.

5.5.1 Database Migration

Database migration is the process of evolving the database schema over time. As your application evolves, you may need to add new tables, modify existing ones, or even change data types. Using migration scripts ensures that your database schema stays in sync with your application's requirements.

Using Migration Tools:

Popular SQL database systems often provide tools for managing database migrations. For example, in PostgreSQL, you can use tools like `pg_dump` and `pg_restore` to create and apply database backups, including schema changes.

Migration Frameworks:

You can also use migration frameworks like Flyway or Liquibase, which offer a structured approach to managing database changes. These frameworks allow you to write migration scripts in SQL or other scripting languages and apply them in a version-controlled manner.

Here's an example of a Flyway migration script in SQL:

```sql
-- V1__Create_Users_Table.sql
CREATE TABLE Users (
    ID SERIAL PRIMARY KEY,
    Username VARCHAR(50) NOT NULL,
    Email VARCHAR(100) UNIQUE,
    CreatedAt TIMESTAMP
);
```

5.5.2 Database Optimization

Optimizing a database involves various techniques to improve performance, reduce resource usage, and enhance the overall efficiency of your database system.

1. Indexing:

Properly indexing frequently queried columns can significantly improve query performance. Use the `CREATE INDEX` statement to create indexes on columns.

2. Query Optimization:

Optimize your SQL queries by using the correct indexing, limiting the use of `SELECT *`, and avoiding complex subqueries whenever possible.

3. Denormalization:

In some cases, denormalizing the database by introducing redundancy can improve query performance. However, this should be done carefully to maintain data consistency.

4. Database Tuning:

Adjust database server parameters like cache size, memory allocation, and thread settings to match your application's requirements.

5. Regular Maintenance:

Perform routine database maintenance tasks like vacuuming, reindexing, and cleaning up unnecessary data.

6. Use Connection Pools:

Connection pools help manage database connections efficiently, reducing the overhead of establishing and closing connections for each request.

7. Caching:

Implement caching mechanisms at both the application and database levels to reduce the need for frequent database queries.

8. Monitoring and Profiling:

Use monitoring tools to track database performance over time and identify bottlenecks or slow queries.

9. Partitioning:

For large tables, consider partitioning data based on specific criteria (e.g., date ranges) to improve query performance.

10. Use Stored Procedures:

Stored procedures can reduce network overhead by executing multiple SQL statements on the database server itself.

11. Regular Backups:

Regularly back up your database to ensure data integrity and quick recovery in case of failures.

12. Security Auditing:

Implement security measures like role-based access control, encryption, and auditing to protect your data.

13. Load Balancing:

Distribute database traffic across multiple database servers to handle high loads effectively.

14. Sharding:

Consider sharding your database to distribute data across multiple servers based on a specific criterion, such as user ID or geographic location.

15. Database Upgrades:

Keep your database system up to date with the latest patches and updates to benefit from performance improvements and security fixes.

In conclusion, database migration and optimization are crucial aspects of maintaining a healthy and efficient SQL database system. Regularly apply migration scripts to adapt to changing requirements, and implement optimization techniques to ensure your database performs at its best. Properly managed databases are essential for the success of modern applications.

CHAPTER VI
Authentication and Security

6.1 Encryption, hashing and salting passwords

Ensuring the security of user passwords is paramount in any application. In this section, we'll explore encryption, hashing, and salting techniques to safeguard user passwords.

6.1.1 Password Encryption

Password encryption involves transforming a plain text password into a cipher text using an encryption algorithm. However, encryption is not suitable for securely storing passwords in databases because it can be reversed (decrypted) if the encryption key is known.

Example of Password Encryption:

```python
import hashlib

from cryptography.fernct import Fernet


# Generate a secret key
key = Fernet.generate_key()

cipher_suite = Fernet(key)
```

Encrypt a password

password = "my_secure_password"

encrypted_password = cipher_suite.encrypt(password.encode())

Store the encrypted password in the database
```



While encryption is useful for securing data in transit, it is not recommended for storing passwords in databases.


## 6.1.2 Password Hashing


Password hashing is the preferred method for securely storing passwords. Hash functions take an input (the password) and produce a fixed-size string of characters, which is unique to that input. Hashing is a one-way process, meaning it's computationally infeasible to reverse it and obtain the original password.


**Example of Password Hashing:**

```python
import hashlib


# Hash a password

password = "my_secure_password"

salt = "random_salt"

hashed_password = hashlib.sha256((password + salt).encode()).hexdigest()
```
```

Store the hashed password and the salt in the database

```
```

In this example, we concatenate the password and a random salt before hashing it. Salting adds an extra layer of security by ensuring that identical passwords result in different hashes due to the unique salt.

6.1.3 Password Salting

Salting involves adding a random value (the salt) to the password before hashing it. Salting ensures that even if two users have the same password, their hashed passwords will be different due to the unique salts.

Example of Password Salting:

```python
import hashlib
import secrets

# Generate a random salt
salt = secrets.token_hex(16)  # 16 bytes (128 bits)

# Hash a password with the salt
password = "my_secure_password"
hashed_password = hashlib.pbkdf2_hmac('sha256', password.encode(), salt.encode(), 100000)
```

Store the hashed password and the salt in the database

```

## 6.1.4 Best Practices

- Use strong and slow hashing algorithms like bcrypt, scrypt, or Argon2 for password hashing.

- Always use a unique salt for each user's password.

- Implement rate limiting and account lockouts to prevent brute-force attacks.

- Periodically update password hashing algorithms and rehash stored passwords.

In summary, password security is vital for protecting user accounts. Hashing passwords with unique salts is a fundamental practice to ensure their security in the event of a data breach. Implementing secure password storage is a cornerstone of authentication and security best practices.
```

6.2 Implementing JWT, OAuth2 for authentication

Authentication is a critical component of application security. In this section, we'll explore the implementation of JWT (JSON Web Tokens) and OAuth2 for user authentication.

6.2.1 JWT (JSON Web Tokens)

JWT is a compact, self-contained way of securely transmitting information between parties as a JSON object. It is commonly used for authentication and authorization in web applications.

Steps to Implement JWT Authentication:

Step 1: Generating JWTs

- When a user logs in, generate a JWT on the server.

- Include user information and a secret key to sign the token.

- Sign the token with a strong algorithm like HMAC SHA256.

```python
import jwt

# Sample user information
user = {"username": "john_doe", "id": 123}
```

```python
# Secret key for signing the token
secret_key = "your_secret_key"


# Generate a JWT
token = jwt.encode(user, secret_key, algorithm="HS256")
```

Step 2: Sending JWT to the Client

- Send the JWT to the client after successful login.

- The client can store the token securely, often in browser cookies or local storage.

Step 3: Verifying JWTs on the Server

- When the client makes subsequent requests, send the JWT in the request header.

- On the server, validate and decode the JWT using the same secret key.

- Ensure the token has not expired and the signature is valid.

```python
try:
    decoded_data = jwt.decode(token, secret_key, algorithms=["HS256"])
    # Access user data from decoded_data
except jwt.ExpiredSignatureError:
```

```
    # Handle token expiration

except jwt.DecodeError:

    # Handle invalid token

```

JWTs are stateless and can be easily scaled, making them a popular choice for securing web applications.

6.2.2 OAuth2

OAuth2 is a widely-used authorization framework that allows applications to access resources on behalf of a user. It's commonly used for third-party authentication (e.g., using Google or Facebook accounts) and securing APIs.

Steps to Implement OAuth2 Authentication:

Step 1: Choose an OAuth2 Provider

- Select an OAuth2 provider (e.g., Google, Facebook, or your custom OAuth2 server).

Step 2: Register Your Application

- Register your application with the OAuth2 provider to obtain client credentials (client ID and client secret).

Step 3: User Authentication

- Redirect the user to the OAuth2 provider's authentication page.

- The user logs in and grants permissions to your application.

Step 4: Obtain an Access Token

- After successful authentication, the OAuth2 provider redirects the user back to your application with an authorization code.

- Your application exchanges the authorization code for an access token.

```python
import requests

# Exchange authorization code for an access token
data = {
    "code": authorization_code,
    "client_id": your_client_id,
    "client_secret": your_client_secret,
    "redirect_uri": your_redirect_uri,
    "grant_type": "authorization_code"
}
response = requests.post(token_url, data=data)
access_token = response.json()["access_token"]
```

```
```

Step 5: Use the Access Token

- Include the access token in API requests to access protected resources.

```python
headers = {"Authorization": "Bearer " + access_token}
response = requests.get(api_url, headers=headers)
```

OAuth2 provides a secure way to authenticate users and authorize third-party applications to access resources without revealing user credentials.

6.2.3 Best Practices

- Keep JWT secret keys secure and rotate them periodically.

- Implement token expiration to enhance security.

- Use HTTPS to encrypt data in transit.

- Regularly audit and monitor OAuth2 applications and their access.

In conclusion, implementing JWT and OAuth2 for authentication is crucial for securing your application and protecting user data. Understanding the intricacies of these authentication mechanisms and following best practices can help ensure a robust security posture for your application.

6.3 Role based authorization and access control

Role-based authorization and access control are fundamental components of application security. In this section, we will discuss how to implement role-based access control (RBAC) to manage user permissions within your application.

6.3.1 Role-Based Access Control (RBAC)

Role-based access control (RBAC) is a security model that restricts system access to authorized users based on their roles. Each user is assigned one or more roles, and each role has specific permissions associated with it. RBAC simplifies access control management by organizing users into logical groups.

Steps to Implement Role-Based Access Control:

Step 1: Define Roles and Permissions

- Identify the different roles that exist within your application (e.g., admin, editor, viewer).

- Define the specific permissions associated with each role (e.g., create, read, update, delete).

Step 2: Assign Roles to Users

- Assign roles to users during registration or as part of user management.

- Store role information in the user's profile or database.

Step 3: Check Permissions

- When a user attempts to perform an action, check their role and permissions.

- Ensure that the user has the required permissions to perform the action.

Example of Role-Based Authorization in Python:

```python
# Sample roles and permissions
roles = {
    "admin": ["create", "read", "update", "delete"],
    "editor": ["create", "read", "update"],
    "viewer": ["read"],
}

# Function to check permissions
def check_permission(user_role, required_permission):
    if user_role in roles:
        if required_permission in roles[user_role]:
            return True
    return False

# Usage
```

```
user_role = "editor"

required_permission = "update"

if check_permission(user_role, required_permission):

    print("User has permission to update.")

else:

    print("User does not have permission to update.")
```

6.3.2 Best Practices

- Implement RBAC at both the application and database levels to ensure comprehensive access control.

- Use a centralized role management system for easy administration.

- Regularly review and update roles and permissions as your application evolves.

- Implement logging and auditing to track user actions and identify security incidents.

- Consider attribute-based access control (ABAC) for fine-grained access control based on user attributes.

6.3.3 Role-Based Access Control in Web Applications

In web applications, RBAC is often implemented by integrating it with the authentication system. Here's a high-level overview of how RBAC can be integrated into a web application:

- During user login, retrieve the user's role(s) from the database.

- Store the user's role(s) in a session or JWT token.

- In your application's controllers or middleware, check the user's role and required permissions before allowing access to specific routes or actions.

- Customize the user interface to display or hide features based on the user's role and permissions.

Role-based access control is a powerful tool for managing user permissions and securing your application. By clearly defining roles and permissions, you can ensure that users only have access to the resources and actions they are authorized to use, enhancing the overall security of your application.

6.4 Securing against SQL injection, XSS, DDoS, etc.

Security is a top priority for any application. In this section, we'll explore common security threats, such as SQL injection, cross-site scripting (XSS), and distributed denial of service (DDoS) attacks, and discuss best practices for mitigating these threats.

6.4.1 SQL Injection

SQL injection is a vulnerability that occurs when untrusted user input is directly included in SQL queries, allowing malicious users to execute arbitrary SQL commands. To prevent SQL injection:

Example of Mitigating SQL Injection in Python (using parameterized queries):

```python
import sqlite3

# Vulnerable query
user_input = "Alice' OR 1=1 --"
query = f"SELECT * FROM users WHERE username = '{user_input}'"

# Mitigated query using parameterized query
query = "SELECT * FROM users WHERE username = ?"
cursor.execute(query, (user_input,))
```

6.4.2 Cross-Site Scripting (XSS)

XSS is an attack where malicious scripts are injected into web pages viewed by other users. To prevent XSS attacks:

Example of Mitigating XSS in HTML (using escaping):

```html
<!-- Vulnerable code -->
<div>Hello, <%= user_input %></div>

<!-- Mitigated code using escaping -->
<div>Hello, <%= escape(user_input) %></div>
```

6.4.3 Distributed Denial of Service (DDoS)

DDoS attacks overwhelm a system by flooding it with traffic. To mitigate DDoS attacks:

- Use a content delivery network (CDN) to distribute traffic and absorb attacks.

- Implement rate limiting and access controls to limit incoming requests.

- Monitor traffic patterns and implement anomaly detection.

6.4.4 Best Practices

- Sanitize and validate user input to prevent injection attacks.

- Use parameterized queries in SQL to separate user input from query logic.

- Implement output encoding or escaping to prevent XSS attacks.

- Regularly update and patch software to fix security vulnerabilities.

- Monitor and log security events to detect and respond to threats.

6.4.5 Web Application Firewalls (WAFs)

Web Application Firewalls (WAFs) are security solutions that protect web applications from various threats, including SQL injection, XSS, and DDoS attacks. WAFs filter incoming traffic and block malicious requests before they reach the application.

Example of Using a WAF (AWS WAF):

- Create rules to block common attack patterns.

- Set rate limiting rules to control request rates.

- Monitor WAF logs for suspicious activity and adjust rules as needed.

```python
# Example AWS WAF rule to block SQL injection
{
  "Action": "block",
```

```json
    "Priority": 1,

    "RuleAction": "COUNT",

    "RuleId": "SQLInjectionRule",

    "Type": "REGEX_MATCH",

    "ExcludedRules": [],

    "Name": "Block SQL Injection",

    "Statement": {

      "ByteMatchStatement": {

        "FieldToMatch": {

          "AllQueryArguments": {}

        },

        "TextTransformations": [

          {

            "Priority": 0,

            "Type": "NONE"

          }

        ],

        "SearchString": "\\b(\\d+)\\s*(['\"()])(?:(?!\\2).)*\\2\\s*=\\s*\\d+"

      }

    }

  }

}
```
```
```

Securing your application against common threats like SQL injection, XSS, and DDoS attacks is crucial to protect user data and maintain service availability. By following best practices and leveraging security tools like WAFs, you can significantly enhance the security posture of your application.

CHAPTER VII
Caching and Performance Optimization

7.1 Caching overview and strategies

Caching is a critical technique to enhance the performance of your application by reducing the time it takes to retrieve and deliver data. In this section, we'll explore caching principles, strategies, and how to implement caching effectively.

7.1.1 What is Caching?

Caching involves storing frequently accessed data in a temporary storage area, such as memory, to accelerate data retrieval. Instead of fetching the data from the original source (e.g., a database or external API) every time, the application can serve it quickly from the cache.

7.1.2 Caching Strategies

1. Page Caching: Cache entire web pages to reduce server load and improve response times for static content. This is suitable for content that doesn't change frequently.

2. Object Caching: Cache individual objects (e.g., database query results, API responses) to reduce the time it takes to retrieve them. Use this for dynamic data that changes infrequently.

3. Fragment Caching: Cache specific parts of a web page, such as a sidebar or a footer. This allows you to cache only the parts of a page that are costly to generate.

4. Content Delivery Network (CDN): Use a CDN to cache and serve static assets (images, CSS, JavaScript) globally, reducing the load on your servers and improving page load times for users worldwide.

7.1.3 Implementing Caching

Example of Implementing Object Caching in Python using Redis:

```python
import redis

# Connect to the Redis server
redis_client = redis.StrictRedis(host='localhost', port=6379, db=0)

# Check if the data is in the cache
cached_data = redis_client.get('my_key')

if cached_data:
    # If data is in the cache, use it
    result = cached_data.decode('utf-8')
else:
    # If data is not in the cache, fetch it from the source
    result = fetch_data_from_source()
```

Store the fetched data in the cache with an expiration time (e.g., 1 hour)

    redis_client.setex('my_key', 3600, result)

```

### 7.1.4 Cache Invalidation and Expiration

To ensure the data in the cache remains up-to-date, implement cache expiration and cache invalidation strategies:

- **Expiration:** Set a time-to-live (TTL) for cached items. When the TTL expires, the cached item is considered stale and needs to be refreshed.

- **Cache Invalidation:** When the underlying data changes (e.g., an update to a database record), invalidate the corresponding cache entry to force a refresh.

### 7.1.5 Monitoring and Optimization

Regularly monitor your caching system to ensure it's working effectively. Measure cache hit rates, response times, and system resource usage. Optimize your caching strategy based on real-world usage patterns.

Caching is a powerful tool for improving the performance and scalability of your application. By understanding caching principles and choosing the right caching strategies, you can significantly enhance your application's responsiveness and reduce the load on your servers.
```

7.2 Implementing caching using Redis, Memcached

Caching is an essential technique to improve the performance of your application. Redis and Memcached are popular in-memory data stores that can be used for caching. In this section, we'll explore how to implement caching using both Redis and Memcached.

7.2.1 Redis

What is Redis?

Redis is an open-source, in-memory data store known for its high performance and versatility. It supports various data structures and is often used as a caching solution.

Implementing Caching with Redis:

1. Installation: First, install Redis on your server and ensure it's running.

2. Client Library: Choose a Redis client library for your programming language (e.g., `redis-py` for Python).

3. Cache Setup: Connect to the Redis server using the client library.

```python
import redis
```

```python
# Connect to Redis

redis_client = redis.StrictRedis(host='localhost', port=6379, db=0)
```

4. Caching Data:

```python
# Check if data is in the cache

cached_data = redis_client.get('my_key')


if cached_data:
    # If data is in the cache, use it
    result = cached_data.decode('utf-8')
else:
    # If data is not in the cache, fetch it from the source
    result = fetch_data_from_source()

    # Store the fetched data in the cache with an expiration time (e.g., 1 hour)
    redis_client.setex('my_key', 3600, result)
```

5. Cache Invalidation and Expiration: Implement cache expiration and invalidation strategies to keep the cache up-to-date.

7.2.2 Memcached

What is Memcached?

Memcached is a high-performance, distributed memory caching system. It's designed for simplicity and speed.

Implementing Caching with Memcached:

1. Installation: Install Memcached on your server and ensure it's running.

2. Client Library: Choose a Memcached client library for your programming language (e.g., `python-memcached` for Python).

3. Cache Setup: Connect to the Memcached server using the client library.

```python
import memcache

# Connect to Memcached
memcached_client = memcache.Client(['localhost:11211'])
```

4. Caching Data:

```python
# Check if data is in the cache

cached_data = memcached_client.get('my_key')


if cached_data is not None:
    # If data is in the cache, use it
    result = cached_data
else:
    # If data is not in the cache, fetch it from the source
    result = fetch_data_from_source()


    # Store the fetched data in the cache with an expiration time (e.g., 1 hour)
    memcached_client.set('my_key', result, time=3600)
```


5. Cache Invalidation and Expiration: Implement cache expiration and invalidation as needed.

7.2.3 Choosing Between Redis and Memcached

- Use Redis if you need more advanced data structures and features like persistence and clustering.

- Use Memcached if you need a simple and lightweight caching solution with minimal configuration.

Both Redis and Memcached are excellent choices for caching, and the decision depends on your specific requirements and familiarity with the technology.

Implementing caching using Redis or Memcached can significantly improve your application's response times and reduce the load on your primary data sources, enhancing overall performance.

7.3 Performance profiling and load testing

Performance profiling and load testing are essential steps in ensuring your backend system can handle real-world usage and deliver the expected performance. In this section, we'll delve into the details of how to profile your application for performance bottlenecks and conduct load testing to assess its scalability.

7.3.1 Performance Profiling

Performance profiling involves analyzing your application to identify performance bottlenecks, such as slow database queries, resource-intensive functions, or inefficient code. Profiling helps pinpoint areas that need optimization.

Steps to Perform Performance Profiling:

1. Select Profiling Tools: Choose a suitable profiling tool for your programming language or platform. Common choices include:

  - For Python: `cProfile`, `Pyflame`, or `Py-Spy`.

  - For Java: `VisualVM`, `YourKit`, or built-in profilers like `jvisualvm`.

  - For Node.js: `clinic`, `node-inspect`, or `ndb`.

2. Instrument Your Code: Integrate the profiling tool into your application code. This usually involves adding profiling statements or configuration to your codebase.

3. Capture Profiling Data: Execute your application while running the profiling tool. It will collect data on the execution time and resource usage of different parts of your code.

4. Analyze the Data: Examine the profiling data to identify bottlenecks and performance issues. Look for functions or methods that consume the most time or resources.

5. Optimize: Once you've identified performance bottlenecks, optimize the corresponding code. This might involve refactoring, improving algorithms, or reducing unnecessary resource usage.

7.3.2 Load Testing

Load testing assesses how your application performs under different levels of concurrent user activity or load. It helps determine whether your system can handle the expected traffic without degradation in performance.

Steps to Perform Load Testing:

1. Define Test Scenarios: Determine the user scenarios and workflows that you want to simulate. These scenarios should represent real-world usage patterns.

2. Select Load Testing Tools: Choose a load testing tool that suits your needs. Popular options include Apache JMeter, Gatling, and locust.io.

3. Create Test Scripts: Develop test scripts that simulate user interactions with your application. These scripts define the user actions, such as browsing pages, making requests, and interacting with forms.

4. Configure Test Parameters: Set up parameters like the number of virtual users, ramp-up time, and test duration. These parameters determine the load applied to your system.

5. Execute Load Tests: Run the load tests using the configured parameters. Monitor system performance, response times, and error rates during the test.

6. Analyze Results: Analyze the test results to identify performance bottlenecks, errors, or degradation under load. Pay attention to response times, throughput, and resource utilization.

7. Optimize and Retest: After identifying issues, make necessary optimizations to your application and repeat the load tests. Continue this process until your system meets performance requirements.

Performance profiling and load testing are ongoing activities that should be conducted regularly as your application evolves. They help ensure that your backend system is robust, scalable, and capable of delivering a responsive experience to users, even under heavy load.

7.4 Scaling databases and servers

Scaling databases and servers is a critical aspect of ensuring that your backend infrastructure can handle increasing traffic and maintain high availability. In this section, we will explore strategies and best practices for scaling both databases and application servers.

7.4.1 Scaling Databases

Scaling a database involves handling more concurrent users, managing larger datasets, and ensuring data consistency while maintaining acceptable response times. Here are the steps to scale your database:

Vertical Scaling:

1. Upgrade Hardware: Start by vertically scaling your database server by upgrading its hardware, such as increasing CPU, RAM, or storage capacity. This is the simplest way to handle increased load initially.

2. Database Optimization: Optimize your database schema, indexes, and queries to improve performance. Identify and eliminate slow-running queries to reduce the load on the database.

Horizontal Scaling:

3. Database Replication: Implement database replication, such as master-slave or master-master replication, to distribute read queries across multiple database instances. This helps offload read traffic from the primary database.

4. Sharding: Consider database sharding to partition your dataset across multiple database servers. Sharding can be based on various criteria, such as customer IDs, geographical regions, or time ranges.

5. Database Clustering: Use database clustering solutions like MySQL Cluster or PostgreSQL streaming replication with Patroni to create high-availability clusters that can handle both reads and writes.

6. Caching: Implement caching layers (e.g., Redis or Memcached) to reduce the load on the database. Cache frequently accessed data to minimize database queries.

7.4.2 Scaling Application Servers

Scaling application servers is essential to handle increased user requests and ensure system reliability. Here's how to scale your application servers:

Horizontal Scaling:

1. Load Balancing: Set up a load balancer in front of your application servers to evenly distribute incoming requests. Popular load balancing solutions include Nginx, HAProxy, and AWS Elastic Load Balancing.

2. Auto-Scaling: Utilize auto-scaling features provided by cloud platforms (e.g., AWS Auto Scaling or Azure Virtual Machine Scale Sets) to automatically add or remove application server instances based on traffic load.

3. Microservices: If applicable, consider transitioning to a microservices architecture, where different parts of your application run in separate containers or server instances. This allows you to scale individual components independently.

4. Caching: Implement caching mechanisms at the application level to store frequently accessed data or HTML fragments. This reduces the load on your application servers and improves response times.

Database Connection Pooling:

5. Database Connection Pooling: Use connection pooling libraries or built-in features of your programming language to manage database connections efficiently. This prevents resource exhaustion and maximizes database utilization.

6. Stateless Services: Design your application servers to be stateless, meaning they don't rely on server-specific session data. Store user sessions and states in a centralized system like Redis or a database.

7. Content Delivery Networks (CDNs): Offload static assets and content to CDNs like Cloudflare or AWS CloudFront. CDNs reduce the load on your application servers and improve content delivery speed.

8. Monitoring and Alerts: Implement robust monitoring and alerting systems to proactively identify performance bottlenecks, server failures, or abnormal behavior.

Scaling databases and servers is an ongoing process that should align with your application's growth. Continuously monitor performance metrics and adjust your scaling strategies as needed to maintain optimal performance and availability.

CHAPTER VIII
Deployment and Maintenance

8.1 Continuous integration and delivery workflows

Continuous Integration (CI) and Continuous Delivery (CD) are crucial practices in modern software development. They help automate the building, testing, and deployment of your applications, ensuring code quality and reducing manual errors. In this section, we will explore CI/CD workflows and how to set them up effectively.

8.1.1 Understanding Continuous Integration (CI)

Continuous Integration is the practice of automatically integrating code changes from multiple contributors into a shared repository multiple times a day. Here are the key steps for setting up CI:

1. Version Control: Use a version control system like Git to manage your codebase. Hosting platforms like GitHub, GitLab, or Bitbucket can help manage repositories and collaboration.

2. Automated Builds: Set up automated build processes that compile your code and create executable artifacts. Popular tools include Jenkins, Travis CI, CircleCI, and GitHub Actions.

3. Unit Testing: Implement unit tests to validate the correctness of your code. CI tools can automatically run these tests whenever new code is pushed, ensuring that changes don't introduce regressions.

4. Code Analysis: Integrate code analysis tools (e.g., SonarQube, ESLint, or Pylint) to enforce coding standards, identify code smells, and detect vulnerabilities.

5. Automated Deployment: While CI focuses on the build and test phases, you can also set up automated deployments to staging environments for further testing.

8.1.2 Implementing Continuous Delivery (CD)

Continuous Delivery extends CI by automating the deployment process, making it possible to release code to production at any time. Here's how to implement CD:

1. Deployment Pipelines: Create deployment pipelines that define the stages and environments your code passes through before reaching production. Common stages include development, testing, staging, and production.

2. Infrastructure as Code (IaC): Use Infrastructure as Code tools like Terraform or AWS CloudFormation to manage your application's infrastructure. This ensures that infrastructure changes are versioned and automated.

3. Containerization: Containerize your applications using Docker to ensure consistency between development and production environments.

4. Orchestration: Use Kubernetes or other container orchestration platforms to manage and scale containers in production.

5. Automated Testing: Implement automated end-to-end tests in your deployment pipeline to verify that your application behaves correctly in the production environment.

6. Manual Approval: Add manual approval gates in your pipeline to allow human intervention before deploying to production.

7. Rollback Mechanism: Set up a rollback mechanism in case of deployment failures or issues discovered in production.

8. Monitoring and Telemetry: Implement comprehensive monitoring and logging to track the health and performance of your applications in real-time.

9. Automated Rollbacks: If issues are detected in production, automate the rollback process to a previously known good state.

10. Continuous Improvement: Continuously improve your CI/CD pipelines based on feedback and lessons learned from each deployment.

By implementing CI/CD, you can accelerate development, reduce the risk of errors, and deliver features and updates to users more quickly and reliably. It fosters a culture of automation and collaboration within your development team, ultimately leading to higher-quality software.

8.2 Containerization using Docker and Kubernetes

Containerization is a critical aspect of modern application deployment, offering a consistent and portable way to package and run applications and their dependencies. Docker and Kubernetes are two popular tools that enable containerization and orchestration. In this section, we'll delve into the specifics of using Docker and Kubernetes for containerization and orchestration.

8.2.1 Docker

Docker Basics

Docker is a platform for developing, shipping, and running applications in containers. Here are the fundamental concepts and steps to get started:

1. **Containers:** Understand what containers are and how they differ from traditional virtualization.

2. **Docker Images:** Learn to create Docker images, which are lightweight, stand-alone, and contain everything needed to run an application, including the code, runtime, libraries, and system tools.

3. **Dockerfile:** Write Dockerfiles to define how images are built. Provide examples of common Dockerfile instructions.

4. **Docker Hub:** Explore Docker Hub, a repository of pre-built Docker images, and how to use it to find and share images.

5. Running Containers: Show how to run containers from images, including options for specifying ports, volumes, and environment variables.

6. Docker Compose: Introduce Docker Compose for defining and running multi-container applications.

8.2.2 Kubernetes

Kubernetes Basics

Kubernetes is an orchestration platform for automating the deployment, scaling, and management of containerized applications. Here's how to work with Kubernetes:

1. Kubernetes Architecture: Explain the components of a Kubernetes cluster, such as the Master Node, Worker Nodes, etcd, and the Kubernetes API.

2. Kubectl: Introduce `kubectl`, the command-line tool for interacting with a Kubernetes cluster. Show how to use it for tasks like deploying applications, inspecting cluster resources, and managing pods.

3. Pods and Deployments: Explain the concept of pods, which are the smallest deployable units in Kubernetes, and how to create and manage them. Introduce Deployments for managing replica sets and scaling applications.

4. Services: Describe Kubernetes Services and how they enable network communication between pods and external clients.

5. ConfigMaps and Secrets: Demonstrate how to manage configuration data and sensitive information using ConfigMaps and Secrets.

6. Ingress: Explore Ingress controllers and rules to manage external access to services within the cluster.

7. Persistent Storage: Discuss Persistent Volumes (PVs) and Persistent Volume Claims (PVCs) for managing storage in Kubernetes.

8. Scaling and Auto-Scaling: Show how to manually scale applications and set up auto-scaling based on resource usage.

9. Logging and Monitoring: Discuss various options and best practices for logging and monitoring Kubernetes applications.

10. Helm Charts: Introduce Helm and Helm Charts as a package manager for Kubernetes applications.

Throughout this section, we'll provide practical examples, command-line snippets, and YAML configurations to help you grasp the essential concepts and hands-on aspects of Docker and Kubernetes. By the end, you should have a solid understanding of containerization and orchestration and be well-prepared to deploy and manage containerized applications in production environments.

8.3 Logging, monitoring and alerting

Effective logging, monitoring, and alerting are essential for ensuring the health and performance of your deployed applications. In this section, we will cover the key aspects of implementing a robust logging, monitoring, and alerting system for your infrastructure and applications.

8.3.1 Logging

Logging Fundamentals

1. Logging Importance: Explain the importance of logging in a production environment, including troubleshooting, auditing, and compliance.

2. Log Levels: Describe various log levels (e.g., DEBUG, INFO, WARNING, ERROR, CRITICAL) and when to use each.

3. Structured Logging: Introduce structured logging and its benefits in aggregating and analyzing log data.

Logging Tools and Best Practices

4. Logging Libraries: Discuss popular logging libraries and frameworks available for different programming languages (e.g., Log4j, Logback, Winston).

5. Log Aggregation: Explain the concept of log aggregation and the role of tools like Elasticsearch, Logstash, and Kibana (ELK stack) or Fluentd and Grafana (EFK stack).

6. Container Logging: Describe how to capture and manage logs from containers using Docker's logging drivers.

7. Centralized Logging: Show how to centralize logs from multiple sources, including applications, servers, and containers, for easier analysis and troubleshooting.

8. Security and Compliance Logging: Discuss the importance of security-related logs for detecting and mitigating security incidents and achieving compliance with regulations.

8.3.2 Monitoring

Monitoring Essentials

1. Monitoring vs. Logging: Differentiate between monitoring and logging and explain their complementary roles.

2. Metrics and Observability: Define key metrics and observability as the ability to understand your system's internal state based on external outputs.

Monitoring Tools and Techniques

3. Monitoring Tools: Introduce popular monitoring tools like Prometheus, Grafana, Nagios, and Datadog, and how they work together.

4. Instrumentation: Discuss the process of instrumenting applications and services to expose relevant metrics.

5. Alerting Rules: Describe how to set up alerting rules to trigger notifications when certain conditions are met.

6. Dashboard Creation: Walk through the creation of custom monitoring dashboards to visualize key metrics and performance indicators.

8.3.3 Alerting

Alerting Strategies

1. Alerting Philosophy: Define the principles of effective alerting, including actionable alerts, avoiding alert fatigue, and setting priorities.

2. Alerting Channels: Discuss different alerting channels, such as email, SMS, chat applications (e.g., Slack), and incident management platforms (e.g., PagerDuty).

Alerting Tools and Configuration

3. Alerting Systems: Explain how to configure alerting systems like Prometheus Alertmanager and integrate them with monitoring tools.

4. Alerting Templates: Provide examples of alerting templates for common scenarios (e.g., high CPU usage, server downtime).

5. Escalation Policies: Discuss the creation of escalation policies for handling alerts and incidents.

8.3.4 Case Studies and Examples

Real-World Scenarios

1. Logging and Monitoring Setup: Walk through a practical example of setting up logging and monitoring for a microservices-based application using the ELK stack and Prometheus-Grafana.

2. Alerting Configuration: Demonstrate how to configure alerting rules and alerting channels for different scenarios, including performance degradation and resource exhaustion.

Throughout this section, we'll provide hands-on guidance, configuration examples, and best practices to help you establish a robust logging, monitoring, and alerting system for your deployment. By the end, you'll be equipped to proactively monitor your infrastructure, troubleshoot issues, and respond to incidents effectively.

8.4 Troubleshooting and debugging techniques

Troubleshooting and debugging are critical skills for maintaining and ensuring the reliability of deployed applications. In this section, we will explore various techniques and best practices for effectively diagnosing and resolving issues in your software and infrastructure.

8.4.1 Troubleshooting Methodology

Understanding the Problem

1. Issue Identification: Discuss how to identify and classify different types of issues, such as performance problems, crashes, or unexpected behavior.

2. Gathering Information: Explain the importance of gathering detailed information about the issue, including error messages, logs, and relevant metrics.

Isolating the Problem

3. Isolation Techniques: Describe methods for isolating issues to specific components, services, or layers of your application stack.

4. Testing Hypotheses: Explore the process of forming hypotheses about the root cause of an issue and testing them systematically.

8.4.2 Debugging Tools and Practices

Debugging Environment Setup

5. Development Environment: Discuss how to set up a debugging-friendly development environment, including code editors, integrated development environments (IDEs), and debugging tools.

Debugging Techniques

6. Logging for Debugging: Explain how to enhance your code with debug-level logging statements to trace program flow and variables' values.

7. Interactive Debugging: Introduce interactive debugging using debugging tools like gdb (GNU Debugger) or integrated debugging features in IDEs.

Performance Profiling

8. Profiling Tools: Describe profiling tools and techniques for identifying performance bottlenecks, including CPU and memory profiling.

9. Load Testing and Benchmarking: Discuss load testing and benchmarking as ways to simulate and analyze performance under different conditions.

8.4.3 Troubleshooting Common Issues

Common Issue Categories

10. Concurrency and Race Conditions: Explain the challenges of concurrency and race conditions and how to detect and resolve them.

11. Memory Leaks: Discuss memory leak detection and resolution strategies.

12. Networking and Connectivity Problems: Address common networking issues such as latency, packet loss, and connectivity problems.

Security and Vulnerability Testing

13. Security Testing: Provide an overview of security testing techniques, including vulnerability scanning and penetration testing.

Case Studies and Examples

14. Real-World Scenarios: Walk through real-world troubleshooting and debugging scenarios, illustrating how to apply the discussed techniques to diagnose and resolve issues.

Throughout this section, we will emphasize hands-on problem-solving, providing practical guidance and examples to help you develop effective troubleshooting and debugging skills. By the end, you will be better equipped to identify, isolate, and resolve issues in your deployed applications and infrastructure.

CHAPTER IX
Web Servers and Deployment Platforms

9.1 Understanding Web Server Technologies (e.g., Apache, Nginx)

In this section, we will delve into the world of web server technologies, focusing on two widely used web servers: Apache HTTP Server and Nginx. Understanding these technologies is crucial for deploying and hosting web applications effectively.

Introduction to Web Servers

1. What is a Web Server: Begin with an explanation of what a web server is and its role in serving web content.

2. Apache HTTP Server:

  - **Overview:** Provide an overview of Apache HTTP Server, its history, and its significance in the web server landscape.

  - **Installation:** Explain how to install and set up Apache on various platforms (Linux, Windows, macOS).

  - **Configuration:** Walk through the basics of configuring Apache, including virtual hosts, modules, and security settings.

  - **Common Use Cases:** Discuss typical use cases for Apache, such as hosting static websites, serving dynamic content through CGI scripts, and acting as a reverse proxy.

3. Nginx:

- **Introduction:** Introduce Nginx as a lightweight and high-performance web server and reverse proxy server.

- **Installation:** Explain how to install and configure Nginx on different platforms.

- **Configuration:** Cover key Nginx configuration directives, including server blocks and location blocks.

- **Load Balancing:** Explore Nginx's load balancing capabilities and its use in distributing traffic among multiple backend servers.

Comparing Apache and Nginx

4. Performance and Scalability: Compare the performance and scalability of Apache and Nginx and discuss scenarios where one might be more suitable than the other.

5. Resource Utilization: Examine how Apache and Nginx differ in terms of resource utilization, memory footprint, and concurrency.

6. Use Cases and Best Practices: Provide guidance on choosing between Apache and Nginx based on specific use cases and best practices.

Security and SSL/TLS

7. Security Considerations: Discuss security best practices for configuring Apache and Nginx to protect against common threats, including DDoS attacks and web application vulnerabilities.

8. SSL/TLS Configuration: Explain how to configure SSL/TLS certificates for secure communication and enable HTTPS on both web servers.

9. Real-World Use Cases: Present real-world examples of how organizations use Apache and Nginx for web hosting, load balancing, and proxying.

10. Hands-On Tutorials: Provide step-by-step tutorials with practical examples and sample configurations to illustrate key concepts.

By the end of this section, you will have a comprehensive understanding of web server technologies, enabling you to make informed decisions when selecting and configuring web servers for hosting and deploying your web applications.

9.2 Deployment Options and Considerations (e.g., Cloud Platforms, On-Premises Servers)

In this section, we will explore various deployment options and considerations when hosting web applications. The choice of deployment platform can significantly impact the scalability, reliability, and performance of your application.

Introduction to Deployment Options

1. Understanding Deployment: Provide an overview of what deployment means in the context of web applications and why it's a critical phase in the development lifecycle.

2. Factors Affecting Deployment: Discuss the factors that influence the choice of deployment platform, including scalability requirements, budget constraints, and geographic distribution.

Deployment on Cloud Platforms

3. Cloud Computing Overview: Introduce cloud computing and its advantages in terms of scalability, flexibility, and cost-effectiveness.

4. Leading Cloud Providers: Discuss major cloud providers like AWS (Amazon Web Services), Azure, and Google Cloud Platform (GCP), highlighting their strengths and differences.

5. Step-by-Step Cloud Deployment:

   - **Selecting a Cloud Provider:** Explain how to choose the most suitable cloud provider for your application.

- **Creating Virtual Machines (VMs):** Walk through the process of provisioning virtual machines on the cloud.

- **Containerization and Orchestration:** Discuss containerization using Docker and orchestration with Kubernetes for efficient cloud deployment.

- **Scaling Strategies:** Explain auto-scaling and load balancing techniques available on cloud platforms.

6. Serverless Computing: Explore the concept of serverless computing and its benefits in terms of reduced operational overhead and cost savings.

On-Premises Deployment

7. On-Premises vs. Cloud: Compare on-premises deployment with cloud-based deployment, highlighting the scenarios where on-premises may be preferred.

8. Hardware and Networking Considerations:

- **Choosing Hardware:** Explain how to select and configure on-premises hardware, including servers and networking equipment.

- **Security:** Discuss security measures for on-premises data centers, including firewalls, intrusion detection, and physical access controls.

Hybrid Deployments

9. Hybrid Cloud: Introduce the concept of hybrid deployments, where organizations combine on-premises infrastructure with cloud resources for flexibility and disaster recovery.

Deployment Best Practices

10. Monitoring and Management: Discuss strategies for monitoring application performance and managing deployments effectively.

11. Backup and Disaster Recovery: Explain backup and disaster recovery planning to ensure data integrity and business continuity.

12. Case Studies: Provide real-world case studies of organizations successfully deploying applications on various platforms.

Conclusion

By the end of this section, you will have a comprehensive understanding of deployment options and considerations, allowing you to make informed decisions about where and how to host your web applications based on your project's specific needs and constraints.

CHAPTER X
API Security

10.1 API Key Authentication

API key authentication is a fundamental security measure used to control access to your APIs by requiring clients to present a valid API key with their requests. In this section, we will delve into the details of API key authentication, its implementation, and best practices.

Understanding API Key Authentication

1. What is an API Key: Explain the concept of API keys and how they are used to authenticate and authorize access to APIs.

2. When to Use API Keys: Discuss scenarios where API key authentication is suitable, such as public APIs or when fine-grained user access control is not required.

API Key Generation and Management

3. Generating API Keys: Describe the process of generating API keys and highlight the importance of strong, unique keys for each client.

4. Key Storage and Security: Discuss best practices for securely storing and managing API keys, including encryption and access control.

5. Server-Side Validation: Explain how the server validates API keys included in incoming requests.

6. Error Handling: Discuss how to handle unauthorized requests and provide appropriate error responses.

Security Best Practices

7. Rate Limiting: Introduce the concept of rate limiting and how it can be combined with API key authentication to mitigate abuse.

8. Key Rotation: Explain the importance of key rotation to enhance security and prevent long-term key abuse.

9. Revoking Keys: Discuss the process of revoking API keys when they are compromised or no longer needed.

Case Studies and Code Examples

10. Practical Examples: Provide code examples in popular programming languages (e.g., Python, Node.js) to illustrate API key authentication implementation.

Testing and Debugging

11. Testing API Key Authentication: Explain how to test your API key authentication mechanism, including tools and techniques for debugging.

Conclusion

By the end of this section, you will have a solid understanding of API key authentication, from its concept to practical implementation, and be equipped to secure your APIs effectively using this method.

10.2 Rate Limiting and Throttling

Rate limiting and throttling are essential strategies to control the usage of your APIs, prevent abuse, and ensure fair and efficient resource allocation. In this section, we will explore rate limiting and throttling techniques, their implementation, and best practices.

Understanding Rate Limiting

1. What is Rate Limiting: Define rate limiting and its significance in API security, highlighting its role in preventing abuse and maintaining API stability.

2. Why Use Rate Limiting: Discuss the scenarios where rate limiting is crucial, such as protecting against DDoS attacks and ensuring a good quality of service.

Rate Limiting Strategies

3. Fixed Window Rate Limiting: Explain the concept of fixed window rate limiting, its benefits, and limitations.

4. Sliding Window Rate Limiting: Introduce sliding window rate limiting as a more flexible approach, and describe its advantages.

5. Token Bucket Algorithm: Discuss the token bucket algorithm as an effective way to implement rate limiting and ensure smooth traffic shaping.

Implementation of Rate Limiting

6. Server-Side Implementation: Describe how to implement rate limiting on the server-side, including data structures and algorithms.

7. Response Headers: Explain how to communicate rate limiting information to clients through response headers.

8. Error Handling: Discuss how to handle rate limit exceeded errors gracefully and provide informative error messages.

Rate Limiting Best Practices

9. Rate Limiting Configuration: Provide guidance on setting appropriate rate limits for different types of APIs and clients.

10. Rate Limiting Headers: Explain how to use headers like `X-RateLimit-Limit` and `X-RateLimit-Remaining` to inform clients about their rate limits.

11. Burst vs. Sustained Rate: Differentiate between burst rate limits (allowing short bursts of requests) and sustained rate limits (long-term rate limits).

12. IP vs. User-Based Rate Limiting: Discuss the pros and cons of IP-based and user-based rate limiting strategies.

Case Studies and Code Examples

13. Practical Examples: Provide code examples in popular programming languages (e.g., Python, Node.js) to demonstrate rate limiting implementation.

14. Testing Rate Limits: Explain how to test your rate limiting mechanisms and monitor their effectiveness.

15. Optimization: Offer optimization tips for enhancing the performance and efficiency of your rate limiting system.

Conclusion

By the end of this section, you will have a comprehensive understanding of rate limiting and throttling techniques, allowing you to effectively implement these strategies to secure and optimize your APIs.

10.3 Cross-Origin Resource Sharing (CORS)

Cross-Origin Resource Sharing (CORS) is a critical security feature implemented by web browsers to control how web pages in one domain can request and consume resources (e.g., APIs) from another domain. Understanding and correctly configuring CORS is crucial for securing your web APIs. In this section, we will delve into CORS in detail, discussing its concepts, implementation, and best practices.

Understanding CORS

1. What is CORS: Explain the concept of CORS, its purpose, and the security risks it mitigates.

2. Same-Origin Policy (SOP): Define the Same-Origin Policy and its limitations that necessitate CORS.

3. Cross-Origin Requests: Describe what cross-origin requests are and the scenarios where they occur.

CORS Implementation

4. CORS Headers: Explore the key HTTP headers involved in CORS, such as `Origin`, `Access-Control-Allow-Origin`, `Access-Control-Allow-Methods`, and `Access-Control-Allow-Headers`.

5. Simple vs. Preflighted Requests: Differentiate between simple and preflighted CORS requests, explaining when each is used.

6. Handling CORS on the Server: Provide code examples in popular server-side programming languages (e.g., Node.js, Python) to demonstrate how to handle CORS requests on the server.

7. Client-Side CORS: Explain how to configure CORS on the client-side, including JavaScript-based solutions and libraries (e.g., Fetch API, Axios).

CORS Best Practices

8. Selective Origins: Discuss the importance of specifying allowed origins explicitly and avoiding overly permissive CORS configurations.

9. Authentication and Cookies: Explain the implications of using cookies and authentication in CORS scenarios.

10. Handling CORS Errors: Provide guidance on how to handle CORS-related errors, including error codes and troubleshooting tips.

Security Considerations

11. Security Implications: Highlight security considerations when configuring CORS, including the risks of overly permissive configurations.

12. Security Headers: Introduce security headers like `Content-Security-Policy` and `X-Content-Type-Options` in the context of CORS.

Case Studies and Practical Examples

13. Real-World Scenarios: Provide real-world examples where CORS is implemented, such as single-page applications (SPAs) consuming APIs.

Testing and Debugging CORS

14. Testing Tools: Recommend tools and techniques for testing and debugging CORS configurations.

Conclusion

By the end of this section, you will have a comprehensive understanding of Cross-Origin Resource Sharing (CORS) and will be equipped to implement it securely to protect your APIs from unauthorized access while enabling legitimate cross-origin requests.

CHAPTER XI
Websockets and Real-Time Communication

11.1 Introduction to Websockets

Websockets have revolutionized how real-time communication is achieved on the web. In this section, we will provide a comprehensive introduction to Websockets, covering their concepts, advantages, and implementation.

Understanding Websockets

1. What are Websockets: Explain the concept of Websockets as a communication protocol that enables full-duplex, bidirectional communication between a client and a server.

2. Key Features: Highlight the key features of Websockets, such as low latency, efficiency, and suitability for real-time applications.

3. HTTP vs. Websockets: Compare Websockets to traditional HTTP requests and explain why Websockets excel in real-time scenarios.

How Websockets Work

4. Handshake Process: Describe the initial handshake process when a Websocket connection is established.

5. Data Frames: Explain how data is sent and received in the form of frames, including text and binary frames.

6. Messaging Patterns: Discuss common messaging patterns used with Websockets, such as one-to-one, one-to-many, and broadcasting.

Websockets in Action

7. Use Cases: Provide real-world examples and use cases where Websockets are the preferred communication technology (e.g., chat applications, online gaming, financial data streaming).

8. Implementing Websockets: Offer code examples in popular programming languages (e.g., JavaScript, Python, Node.js) to demonstrate how to create a basic Websocket server and client.

Websocket Libraries and Frameworks

9. Available Libraries: Introduce popular libraries and frameworks for working with Websockets (e.g., Socket.IO, WebSocket API).

Handling Websocket Security

10. Security Considerations: Discuss security concerns associated with Websockets, such as denial-of-service attacks and data validation.

11. Securing Websockets: Provide best practices and security measures for securing Websockets, including authentication and authorization.

Conclusion

By the end of this section, you will have a solid understanding of Websockets and their role in enabling real-time communication on the web. You'll also be equipped with the knowledge to implement Websockets securely in your applications.

11.2 Building Real-Time Features in Back-End Applications

In this section, we will delve into the practical aspects of building real-time features in back-end applications using Websockets. We'll explore the steps involved, provide code examples, and guide you through the process.

Setting Up a Back-End Websocket Server

1. Choosing a Technology Stack: Discuss popular programming languages and frameworks (e.g., Node.js with Socket.IO, Python with Tornado) for building back-end Websocket servers.

2. Project Structure: Explain how to organize your project and files to facilitate real-time features.

3. Creating a Websocket Server: Provide a step-by-step guide on setting up a Websocket server using your chosen technology stack.

Real-Time Use Cases

4. Chat Application: Walk through the development of a real-time chat application as an example use case. Include code snippets for both the server and client sides.

5. Live Notifications: Explain how to implement live notifications or updates in an application, such as real-time news feeds or notifications in a social media app.

6. Collaborative Editing: Explore the development of collaborative features like real-time document editing or collaborative drawing boards.

Scaling and Load Balancing

7. Scaling Considerations: Discuss strategies for scaling your Websocket server to handle a large number of simultaneous connections.

8. Load Balancing: Explain how load balancing can be used to distribute incoming Websocket connections across multiple server instances.

Security in Real-Time Applications

9. Authentication and Authorization: Describe how to implement user authentication and authorization mechanisms to secure your real-time features.

10. Data Validation: Discuss the importance of data validation and sanitization to prevent security vulnerabilities.

Handling Failures and Errors

11. Error Handling: Provide guidance on handling errors gracefully in real-time applications and dealing with issues like dropped connections.

Testing and Debugging

12. Testing Real-Time Features: Explain testing approaches and tools for real-time features, including unit testing and integration testing.

13. Debugging Techniques: Offer tips and techniques for debugging real-time applications and diagnosing common issues.

Conclusion

By the end of this section, you will have a comprehensive understanding of how to build real-time features in back-end applications using Websockets. You'll be equipped with the knowledge and practical skills to implement these features in your own projects, ensuring they are efficient, secure, and robust.

11.3 Handling WebSocket Security

Ensuring the security of your WebSocket-based real-time communication is paramount. In this section, we will explore various security considerations and best practices when dealing with WebSocket implementations.

Authentication and Authorization

1. User Authentication: Describe how to implement user authentication for WebSocket connections. You can use techniques like token-based authentication or session cookies.

2. Authorization: Explain the importance of proper authorization mechanisms. Describe how to restrict access to specific WebSocket channels or features based on user roles or permissions.

3. Securing Authentication Credentials: Provide guidance on securing user credentials during WebSocket authentication. Discuss best practices for storing and transmitting sensitive information.

Data Validation and Sanitization

4. Input Validation: Explain the importance of validating and sanitizing incoming data to prevent security vulnerabilities, such as injection attacks.

5. Message Validation: Describe how to validate WebSocket messages, ensuring they conform to expected formats and structures.

Cross-Origin Security (CORS)

6. CORS Overview: Introduce Cross-Origin Resource Sharing (CORS) and why it's important in WebSocket security.

7. Implementing CORS: Provide practical examples and code snippets on how to implement CORS policies to control which origins are allowed to connect to your WebSocket server.

Encryption and Transport Layer Security (TLS)

8. Securing WebSocket Connections: Explain how to secure WebSocket connections using Transport Layer Security (TLS) to encrypt data in transit.

9. Obtaining and Managing SSL/TLS Certificates: Offer guidance on obtaining and managing SSL/TLS certificates for your WebSocket server.

Protection Against Common Attacks

10. Securing Against WebSocket Injections: Discuss strategies to protect your WebSocket server against injection attacks like Cross-Site Scripting (XSS) and SQL Injection.

11. Rate Limiting and Throttling: Explain how rate limiting and throttling can help protect your server from abuse or Distributed Denial of Service (DDoS) attacks.

Logging and Monitoring

12. Logging Security Events: Describe the importance of logging security-related events and how it can aid in identifying and mitigating security issues.

13. Security Checklist: Summarize the security best practices discussed throughout the chapter in a checklist format.

Conclusion

By the end of this section, you will have a comprehensive understanding of how to secure WebSocket-based real-time communication. You'll be equipped with the knowledge and tools to protect your applications from common security threats and vulnerabilities, ensuring the privacy and integrity of your real-time data.

CHAPTER XII
Microservices and Service-Oriented Architecture (SOA)

12.1 Understanding microservices

Microservices architecture is a software design approach where a single application is built as a suite of small, independent services that communicate with each other through well-defined APIs. In this section, we will delve into the key concepts and principles of microservices.

Definition of Microservices

1. What Are Microservices: Define microservices and explain the fundamental concept behind breaking down monolithic applications into smaller, manageable services.

Benefits and Advantages

2. Scalability: Describe how microservices enable horizontal scaling and flexibility in resource allocation.

3. Technology Heterogeneity: Explain how microservices allow different services to be built with different technologies and programming languages.

4. Independent Development: Highlight the advantages of independent development and deployment cycles for microservices.

5. Improved Fault Isolation: Discuss how microservices can isolate faults to prevent cascading failures.

Challenges and Considerations

6. Complexity Management: Discuss the challenges of managing a distributed system of microservices and strategies to address complexity.

7. Service Communication: Explain how microservices communicate with each other and the importance of robust communication mechanisms.

8. Data Management: Discuss challenges related to data consistency, storage, and databases in a microservices environment.

Use Cases and Examples

9. Real-World Use Cases: Provide real-world examples of companies that have successfully adopted microservices and the benefits they've achieved.

Implementing Microservices with Back-End Technologies

10. Technology Stack: Discuss common back-end technologies and frameworks used for building microservices.

11. Design Principles: Explain key design principles such as the Single Responsibility Principle (SRP), separation of concerns, and the importance of well-defined APIs.

12. Communication Protocols: Describe commonly used communication protocols and patterns like RESTful APIs, GraphQL, and message queues.

13. Containerization and Orchestration: Introduce containerization with Docker and orchestration with Kubernetes as tools for managing microservices.

14. Scaling Microservices: Discuss strategies for scaling microservices both horizontally and vertically.

Conclusion

By the end of this section, you will have a solid understanding of what microservices are, their benefits, challenges, and the technologies and practices involved in implementing them. This knowledge will lay the foundation for effectively designing and building microservices-based applications.

12.2 Benefits and Challenges of Microservices

Microservices architecture offers several benefits and advantages, but it also comes with its set of challenges that organizations need to consider when adopting it.

Benefits of Microservices

1. Scalability: Microservices allow for independent scaling of individual services. This means you can allocate resources precisely where they are needed, enhancing efficiency and cost-effectiveness.

2. Technology Heterogeneity: With microservices, you can use different technologies and programming languages for different services. This flexibility allows you to choose the best tool for each job.

3. Independent Development: Each microservice can be developed, tested, and deployed independently. This accelerates development cycles and allows teams to work on different services concurrently.

4. Improved Fault Isolation: Microservices are isolated from one another, reducing the risk of a failure in one service cascading to others. This improves system reliability.

5. Enhanced Maintainability: Smaller codebases and independent services are easier to maintain and update. This makes it simpler to add new features or fix issues without affecting the entire system.

Challenges and Considerations

6. Complexity Management: The distributed nature of microservices can introduce complexity in terms of service discovery, load balancing, and inter-service communication. Strategies like service mesh can help manage this complexity.

7. Service Communication: Microservices communicate over networks, which can introduce latency and network-related failures. Proper design and use of communication protocols are crucial.

8. Data Management: Handling data consistency and managing databases in a microservices architecture can be challenging. Techniques like database per service and event-driven architectures can address these challenges.

9. Deployment and Orchestration: Coordinating the deployment and scaling of multiple microservices can be complex. Containerization and orchestration tools like Docker and Kubernetes can simplify this process.

10. Testing and Debugging: Testing microservices individually and as a whole can be challenging. Techniques like contract testing and distributed tracing can aid in debugging and ensuring the integrity of the system.

Use Cases and Examples

11. Real-World Use Cases: Provide examples of organizations that have successfully adopted microservices, showcasing the benefits they've reaped and how they addressed challenges.

Conclusion

Understanding the benefits and challenges of microservices is essential for organizations considering this architectural approach. By weighing the advantages against the complexities

and challenges, businesses can make informed decisions about adopting microservices to meet
their specific needs.

12.3 Implementing Microservices with Back-End Technologies

Implementing microservices involves breaking down a monolithic application into smaller, independently deployable services. These services communicate with each other through APIs or message queues. Below, we'll explore how to implement microservices using common back-end technologies.

Choosing a Programming Language and Framework

1. Selecting a Language: Begin by choosing a programming language suitable for your microservices. Popular languages include Java, Python, Node.js, and Go.

2. Choosing a Framework: Depending on the language you choose, select a microservices framework that simplifies development and provides features like service discovery and communication. Examples include Spring Boot for Java, Flask for Python, and Express.js for Node.js.

Service Design and Architecture

3. Define Service Boundaries: Identify clear boundaries for your microservices. Each service should have a specific responsibility or domain, such as user management or product catalog.

4. API Design: Design clear and well-documented APIs for your microservices. RESTful APIs with JSON payloads are common, but GraphQL is another option for more flexible querying.

Communication Between Microservices

5. HTTP/HTTPS: Microservices often communicate via HTTP/HTTPS RESTful APIs. Ensure that services can securely call each other using these protocols.

6. Message Queues: Use message queuing systems like RabbitMQ or Apache Kafka for asynchronous communication between microservices. This decouples services and improves scalability.

Data Management

7. Database Per Service: Consider a database per microservice. Each service manages its database, reducing contention and making it easier to scale independently.

8. Event Sourcing: Event sourcing can be beneficial for certain scenarios where you need to capture and track changes to data over time.

Containerization and Orchestration

9. Containerization: Containerize your microservices using Docker. Containers encapsulate services, making them easy to deploy consistently across different environments.

10. Orchestration: Use container orchestration platforms like Kubernetes to manage and scale your containers. Kubernetes simplifies tasks like load balancing, service discovery, and scaling.

Testing and Continuous Integration/Continuous Deployment (CI/CD)

11. Unit Testing: Write unit tests for each microservice to ensure they function correctly in isolation.

12. Integration Testing: Test how microservices interact with each other. Tools like Postman and Newman can help automate API testing.

13. CI/CD Pipeline: Set up a CI/CD pipeline to automate testing, building, and deploying microservices to various environments (development, staging, production).

Monitoring and Logging

14. Monitoring: Implement monitoring solutions like Prometheus, Grafana, or application performance monitoring (APM) tools to track the health and performance of your microservices.

15. Logging: Use structured logging to collect and centralize logs. Tools like ELK Stack (Elasticsearch, Logstash, Kibana) can help with log analysis.

Security

16. API Security: Implement security measures like OAuth 2.0, JWT authentication, and API gateways to protect your microservices.

17. Container Security: Ensure the security of your Docker containers by regularly updating base images and scanning for vulnerabilities.

Scaling

18. Horizontal Scaling: Utilize horizontal scaling to add more instances of a microservice to handle increased load.

19. Load Balancing: Implement load balancing to distribute traffic evenly across multiple instances of a microservice.

Conclusion

Implementing microservices with back-end technologies involves careful planning, architectural design, and selecting the right tools and practices. By following these steps and considering the unique needs of your application, you can successfully build and deploy microservices to achieve scalability and maintainability.

CHAPTER XIII
Version Control Best Practices

13.1 Advanced Git Techniques (e.g., Branching Strategies, Rebasing)

Git is a powerful version control system that allows for advanced techniques and workflows to streamline development and collaboration. In this section, we'll explore some advanced Git techniques that can enhance your version control practices.

Branching Strategies

1. Feature Branches: Use feature branches to develop new features or fix issues. Create a new branch for each feature or bug fix. This isolates changes and allows for parallel development.

```bash
git checkout -b feature/my-feature
```

2. Release Branches: Create release branches to prepare for a new release. It's a stable branch where you can perform bug fixes and prepare the release.

```bash
git checkout -b release/1.0
```

3. Hotfix Branches: When critical issues arise in production, create hotfix branches from the release branch to fix them. Merge the fix into both the release and main branches.

```bash
git checkout -b hotfix/1.0.1 release/1.0
```

4. Git Flow: Consider adopting Git Flow, a branching model that defines branch naming and usage conventions. It formalizes feature, release, and hotfix branches.

Interactive Rebasing

5. Interactive Rebasing: Interactive rebasing allows you to modify commit history before pushing it. This can be useful for cleaning up, reordering, or combining commits.

```bash
git rebase -i HEAD~3  # Rebase the last 3 commits interactively
```

6. Squashing Commits: Squash multiple commits into one to make commit history cleaner. Interactive rebasing allows you to combine commits.

Managing Remote Repositories

7. Forking Workflow: If collaborating on open-source projects, fork the repository first. Clone your fork locally and create feature branches.

```bash
git clone <your-fork-url>
```

8. Pull Requests: When ready to contribute, create a pull request from your feature branch to the original repository. This facilitates code review and integration.

Stashing Changes

9. Stash Changes: Use `git stash` to temporarily save changes when you need to switch branches or perform other actions without committing incomplete work.

```bash
git stash save "Work in progress"
```

10. Apply Stash: Retrieve stashed changes later using `git stash apply` or `git stash pop` to apply and remove the stash.

```bash
git stash apply stash@{0}
```

Conclusion

Advanced Git techniques like branching strategies and interactive rebasing can significantly improve your version control workflow. These practices help keep your codebase organized, simplify collaboration, and ensure a clean commit history. By mastering these techniques, you'll become a more proficient Git user and developer.

13.2 Collaborative Development Workflows

Collaborative development workflows are essential for teams working together on software projects. In this section, we'll explore several collaborative workflows and best practices for effective teamwork using Git.

Centralized Workflow

The centralized workflow is suitable for small teams and organizations. It revolves around a single, central repository. Developers clone this repository, make changes, and push them back.

1. Clone the Repository: Each developer clones the central repository to their local machine.

```bash
git clone <repository-url>
```

2. Create Feature Branches: Developers create feature branches for their work.

```bash
git checkout -b feature/my-feature
```

3. Commit Changes: Developers commit their changes to their feature branches.

```bash
```

```bash
git commit -m "Implemented feature XYZ"
```

4. Push Changes: Push changes to the central repository.

```bash
git push origin feature/my-feature
```

5. Pull Requests: Developers create pull requests (or merge requests) to propose changes. Code review and discussion happen in these requests.

Feature Branch Workflow

The feature branch workflow is an extension of the centralized workflow. It encourages developers to use branches for features and bug fixes.

1. Create Feature Branches: Developers create feature branches for their work.

```bash
git checkout -b feature/my-feature
```

2. Commit Changes: Developers commit changes to their feature branches.

```bash
git commit -m "Implemented feature XYZ"
```

3. Pull Latest Changes: Periodically, developers pull the latest changes from the central repository to keep their feature branches up to date.

```bash
git pull origin main
```

4. Push Changes: Once the feature is complete, push the feature branch and create a pull request.

```bash
git push origin feature/my-feature
```

5. Code Review: Team members review the code, suggest changes, and discuss improvements.

Forking Workflow

The forking workflow is suitable for open-source projects or larger teams. Developers fork the central repository, clone their forks, and propose changes through pull requests.

1. Fork the Repository: Developers fork the central repository on the platform (e.g., GitHub, GitLab).

2. Clone Your Fork: Clone your fork to your local machine.

```bash
git clone <your-fork-url>
```

3. Create Feature Branches: Create feature branches for your work.

```bash
git checkout -b feature/my-feature
```

4. Commit and Push Changes: Commit changes to your feature branch and push it to your fork.

```bash
git commit -m "Implemented feature XYZ"
git push origin feature/my-feature
```

5. Pull Requests: Create a pull request from your feature branch to the central repository. Project maintainers review and merge the changes.

These collaborative development workflows help teams manage changes, coordinate development efforts, and maintain code quality in a structured manner. Choose the workflow that best fits your project's size and complexity.

CHAPTER XIV
Internationalization and Localization

14.1 Making Back-End Applications Multilingual

In today's globalized world, making your back-end applications multilingual is crucial to reach a wider audience. This section will guide you through the process of internationalizing your back-end application to support multiple languages.

1. Identify Texts to Translate

Before you start, identify all the text elements in your back-end application that need to be translated. This includes error messages, labels, notifications, and any dynamic content generated by your application.

2. Choose a Framework or Library

Select a framework or library that provides internationalization (i18n) support for your programming language. Common choices include:

- **Node.js:** Use libraries like `i18next` or `node-i18n`.

- **Python:** Django and Flask have built-in i18n support.

- **Ruby:** Ruby on Rails has i18n support.

- **Java:** Use the Java Internationalization (Java i18n) API.

- **PHP:** PHP's `gettext` extension is a popular choice.

3. Organize Translations

Create language-specific files or dictionaries that store translations for each supported language. Typically, these files are in a key-value format.

For example, in a Node.js application using `i18next`, you might have translation files like `en.json` and `fr.json`:

```json
// en.json
{
  "greeting": "Hello!",
  "error": "An error occurred."
}

// fr.json
{
  "greeting": "Bonjour !",
  "error": "Une erreur s'est produite."
}
```

4. Implement Localization in Code

Use the chosen library or framework to replace static text in your code with references to the translation files. Here's an example in Node.js using `i18next`:

```javascript
const i18next = require('i18next');

const i18nextMiddleware = require('i18next-http-middleware');

i18next.init({
  lng: 'en', // Default language
  resources: {
    en: {
      translation: require('./locales/en.json'),
    },
    fr: {
      translation: require('./locales/fr.json'),
    },
  },
});

app.use(i18nextMiddleware.handle(i18next));

// Usage in code
```

```
const greeting = req.t('greeting'); // Automatically translates based on the user's language preference
```

5. Detect User's Language

Implement a mechanism to detect the user's preferred language. This can be done through browser settings, user preferences, or user accounts.

6. Test Thoroughly

Thoroughly test your multilingual application to ensure that translations are correctly displayed and that the user experience is consistent across languages. Pay attention to text expansion and contraction, which can affect layout.

7. Maintain and Update Translations

Regularly update and maintain your translation files as your application evolves. Consider involving native speakers or professional translators to ensure quality translations.

By following these steps, you can make your back-end application multilingual, making it more accessible and user-friendly to a global audience. This approach enables users to interact with your application in their preferred language, enhancing their experience.

14.2 Handling Date, Time, and Currency Formats for Different Locales

Handling date, time, and currency formats is an essential aspect of internationalization (i18n) and localization (l10n) for back-end applications. Different regions have varying conventions for displaying these formats, so it's crucial to adapt your application accordingly.

1. Use Locale-Specific Libraries

Most programming languages provide libraries or functions to format dates, times, and currencies according to the user's locale. Utilize these built-in features to ensure correctness and consistency. Here are examples in different languages:

- JavaScript (Node.js):

```javascript
const date = new Date();
const formattedDate = date.toLocaleDateString('en-US'); // Specify the desired locale
```

- Python:

```python
import datetime
import locale

# Set the desired locale
locale.setlocale(locale.LC_TIME, 'en_US.UTF-8')
```

```python
date = datetime.datetime.now()
formatted_date = date.strftime('%x')  # Format according to locale
```

- **Java:**

```java
import java.util.Date;
import java.text.DateFormat;
import java.util.Locale;


Date date = new Date();
Locale locale = new Locale("en", "US"); // Specify the desired locale
DateFormat dateFormat = DateFormat.getDateInstance(DateFormat.DEFAULT, locale);
String formattedDate = dateFormat.format(date);
```

- **PHP:**

```php
$date = new DateTime();
$date->setLocale('en_US'); // Specify the desired locale
$formattedDate = $date->format('F j, Y'); // Format according to locale
```

2. User Locale Detection

Detect the user's preferred locale either through user preferences or browser settings. You can use this information to dynamically set the locale for formatting. Many web frameworks and libraries provide mechanisms for this.

3. Maintain Locale-Specific Data

Ensure that your application has access to locale-specific data, such as date and time formatting patterns and currency symbols. You can store this data in configuration files or use language packs provided by localization libraries.

4. Formatting Examples

When displaying dates, times, or currency, use the appropriate formatting functions or methods based on the detected or selected locale. Here are examples of date and currency formatting:

- **Date Formatting:**

  - `MM/dd/yyyy` (U.S. locale)

  - `dd/MM/yyyy` (European locale)

  - `yyyy-MM-dd` (ISO 8601 format)

- **Currency Formatting:**

  - `$1,000.00` (U.S. locale)

  - `€1.000,00` (European locale)

  - `¥1,000.00` (Japanese locale)

By following these steps and using locale-specific libraries, you can ensure that your back-end application formats dates, times, and currencies correctly for different locales. This enhances the user experience and makes your application more accessible to a global audience.

CHAPTER XV
Getting Started

15.1 Overview of Serverless Architecture

Serverless architecture, often referred to as Functions-as-a-Service (FaaS), is a cloud computing model that abstracts server management away from developers. In this model, you can focus solely on writing and deploying code (functions) without dealing with the underlying infrastructure. Here, we'll provide a detailed overview of serverless architecture.

Key Concepts in Serverless Architecture

1. Functions as Units: Serverless computing revolves around functions. Functions are individual units of code that perform specific tasks. You define functions, and the cloud provider automatically manages their execution.

2. Event-Driven: Functions in a serverless environment are triggered by events. These events can be HTTP requests, database updates, file uploads, or other types of events depending on your cloud provider.

3. Stateless: Serverless functions are typically stateless. They don't maintain server-side state between invocations. Any required state must be managed externally, often through databases or storage services.

4. Automatic Scaling: One of the main advantages of serverless is automatic scaling. The cloud provider automatically provisions resources to handle incoming requests, ensuring that your application can handle any load.

5. Pay-Per-Use Pricing: With serverless, you only pay for the actual compute time consumed by your functions. There are no upfront costs or charges for idle resources.

Common Use Cases

Serverless architecture is well-suited for various use cases, including:

- **APIs:** You can create RESTful APIs or GraphQL APIs using serverless functions. These functions handle HTTP requests and can be easily scaled to accommodate traffic spikes.

- **Data Processing:** Serverless is excellent for data processing tasks like image or video transcoding, data transformations, and log processing.

- **IoT:** Handling events from Internet of Things (IoT) devices is a common use case. Serverless functions can process sensor data, perform real-time analysis, and trigger actions.

- **Background Jobs:** Long-running background jobs like sending emails, generating reports, and cleaning up databases can be efficiently handled with serverless.

Serverless Providers

There are several cloud providers offering serverless platforms. Some of the most popular ones include:

- **AWS Lambda:** Amazon Web Services' serverless offering is AWS Lambda. It supports multiple programming languages and integrates with various AWS services.

- **Azure Functions:** Microsoft's Azure Functions allows you to build serverless applications using .NET, Node.js, Python, and more. It offers tight integration with Azure services.

- **Google Cloud Functions**: Google Cloud Functions enables serverless computing on Google Cloud Platform. It supports multiple languages and integrates with other GCP services.

- **IBM Cloud Functions:** IBM Cloud provides its serverless platform called IBM Cloud Functions, which supports Node.js, Python, Swift, and more.

Benefits of Serverless Architecture

- **Scalability:** Automatic scaling ensures your application can handle varying workloads.

- **Cost-Effective:** Pay-per-use pricing means you only pay for what you use.

- **Reduced Operational Overhead:** Serverless abstracts infrastructure management tasks, reducing operational complexity.

- **Faster Development:** Focusing on writing functions allows for rapid development and deployment.

- **Elasticity:** Serverless is well-suited for bursty workloads that require quick scaling.

Challenges

- **Cold Starts:** There can be a latency penalty for infrequently used functions due to cold starts.

- **Limited Execution Time:** Functions typically have a maximum execution time, which may not be suitable for long-running tasks.

- **Vendor Lock-In:** Serverless platforms are not entirely portable, so there's a degree of vendor lock-in.

Serverless architecture offers numerous benefits for specific use cases but may not be suitable for all applications. Understanding its principles and how to leverage it effectively is essential for building efficient and cost-effective cloud applications.

15.2 Deploying Functions in a Serverless Environment (e.g., AWS Lambda, Azure Functions)

In this section, we'll explore how to deploy functions in a serverless environment, with a focus on two popular cloud providers: AWS Lambda and Azure Functions. We'll provide step-by-step guidance on deploying serverless functions, including code examples and explanations.

AWS Lambda

Step 1: Create a Lambda Function

1. Log in to your AWS Management Console and navigate to AWS Lambda.

2. Click "Create function."

3. Choose "Author from scratch" or use a predefined blueprint.

4. Configure your function by specifying a name, runtime (e.g., Node.js, Python), and execution role.

5. Click "Create function."

Step 2: Write and Upload Code

1. In the Lambda function editor, you can write code inline or upload a ZIP package with your code files.

2. Ensure your code includes a handler function that Lambda can execute.

3. Set environment variables or other configuration settings if needed.

Step 3: Configure Triggers

1. Choose a trigger for your Lambda function. This can be an API Gateway, an S3 bucket, or other AWS services.

2. Configure trigger-specific settings, such as event sources or HTTP endpoints.

Step 4: Test Your Function

1. Use the Lambda console to test your function. You can provide sample input data for testing.

Step 5: Deploy Your Function

1. Once you're satisfied with your function, click "Deploy."

2. Your Lambda function is now live and can be invoked based on its triggers.

Azure Functions

Step 1: Create an Azure Function

1. Log in to your Azure portal and navigate to Azure Functions.

2. Click "New Function App" to create a new function app.

3. Configure your function app settings, including the runtime stack (e.g., Node.js, C#), hosting plan, and storage account.

4. Click "Create" to create the function app.

Step 2: Write and Upload Code

1. In the Azure Functions portal, navigate to your function app.

2. Click "+ New Function" to create a new function.

3. Write your code in the integrated code editor or upload code files.

4. Specify the trigger for your function, such as an HTTP trigger or a timer trigger.

Step 3: Configure Triggers and Bindings

1. Azure Functions use bindings to connect to data sources and triggers. Configure these bindings in your function code.

Step 4: Test Your Function

1. Use the Azure Functions portal to test your function with sample input data.

Step 5: Deploy Your Function

1. After testing, your function is ready to be deployed. Click "Deploy" or use Azure DevOps for CI/CD pipelines.

2. Your Azure Function is now live and can be triggered based on its configured triggers.

Deploying functions in a serverless environment simplifies infrastructure management and enables efficient scaling. Whether you choose AWS Lambda or Azure Functions, understanding the deployment process is crucial for building and maintaining serverless applications effectively.

Appendix A
Sample Projects and Code Examples

In this appendix, we will provide you with a selection of sample projects and code examples to reinforce the concepts discussed throughout this guide. These examples cover various aspects of back-end development, including authentication, database interaction, API creation, and more. Each example comes with step-by-step instructions and explanations.

1. User Authentication with Node.js and Express

Learn how to implement user authentication using Node.js and Express. This example covers user registration, login, password hashing, and session management.

- Create a new Node.js project.

- Set up an Express server.

- Implement user registration and login routes.

- Use bcrypt for password hashing.

- Manage user sessions with Express sessions.

2. RESTful API Development with Python and Flask

Build a RESTful API using Python and Flask. You'll create endpoints for CRUD (Create, Read, Update, Delete) operations on a resource.

- Set up a Flask project.

- Define routes and handlers for different HTTP methods (GET, POST, PUT, DELETE).

- Use SQLAlchemy for database interactions.

- Implement authentication and authorization for API endpoints.

3. Real-time Chat Application with Websockets

Create a real-time chat application using Websockets. This example will show you how to establish Websocket connections, handle messages, and broadcast updates to connected clients.

- Set up a Node.js server with the WebSocket library.

- Create a basic chat UI with HTML and JavaScript.

- Handle WebSocket connections and messages.

- Broadcast messages to all connected clients in real-time.

4. Serverless Function for Image Processing (AWS Lambda)

Develop a serverless function on AWS Lambda to process images. This example demonstrates how to trigger a Lambda function when an image is uploaded to an S3 bucket.

- Create a Lambda function using the AWS Lambda console.

- Set up an S3 bucket for image storage.

- Configure an S3 trigger to invoke the Lambda function on image uploads.

- Write Node.js code to process and resize images.

5. Dockerizing a Node.js Application

Dockerize a Node.js application for containerized deployment. This example guides you through creating a Dockerfile and running your app in a Docker container.

- Write a Dockerfile for your Node.js application.

- Build a Docker image.

- Run and manage Docker containers.

- Explore Docker Compose for multi-container applications.

These sample projects and code examples are designed to provide hands-on experience and reinforce your understanding of back-end development concepts. Feel free to use them as starting points for your own projects or experiments.

Remember that learning by doing is often the most effective way to gain proficiency in back-end development, so don't hesitate to dive in and start coding!

Appendix B
Recommended Tools and Resources

In this appendix, we'll provide you with a list of recommended tools and resources that can be incredibly valuable for back-end development. These tools cover a range of categories, from code editors and version control systems to online courses and documentation. Additionally, we'll include brief explanations of each tool's purpose and benefits.

1. Integrated Development Environments (IDEs)

- **Visual Studio Code (VS Code):** A free, open-source code editor developed by Microsoft. It offers extensive extensions for various programming languages and excellent debugging support.

- **PyCharm:** An IDE specifically designed for Python development, offering features like code completion, a powerful debugger, and integration with popular web frameworks.

- **IntelliJ IDEA:** A versatile Java IDE that supports multiple languages and frameworks, including Spring, Kotlin, and JavaScript.

2. Version Control

- **Git:** The most widely used distributed version control system. It's essential for tracking changes, collaborating with others, and managing code repositories.

- **GitHub:** A web-based platform for hosting and collaborating on Git repositories. It provides features like issue tracking, pull requests, and project management.

- **GitLab:** An alternative to GitHub, GitLab offers both cloud-hosted and self-hosted solutions. It includes built-in continuous integration and container registry features.

3. Database Management

- **MySQL Workbench:** A visual database design tool for MySQL databases, allowing you to create and manage databases with ease.

- **PostgreSQL:** An open-source relational database management system known for its advanced features and support for JSON data.

- **MongoDB Compass:** A graphical user interface for MongoDB, making it easier to interact with NoSQL databases.

4. API Development and Testing

- **Postman:** A popular API testing tool that simplifies the process of building, testing, and documenting APIs.

- **Swagger:** A tool for designing, building, and documenting RESTful APIs, ensuring consistency and ease of use.

- **Insomnia:** An open-source API client that helps developers test and debug APIs with features like code generation and scripting.

5. Documentation and Collaboration

- **Swagger UI:** A user-friendly interface for visualizing and interacting with Swagger-documented APIs.

- **Confluence:** A collaboration tool that helps teams create, share, and collaborate on projects, including technical documentation.

- **Notion:** A versatile workspace for creating documents, wikis, and knowledge bases, suitable for documenting code and processes.

6. Learning Resources

- **Udemy:** An online learning platform with a wide range of back-end development courses, often covering specific technologies and frameworks.

- **edX:** Offers courses from top universities and institutions on various back-end development topics.

- **Stack Overflow:** An invaluable resource for troubleshooting, learning, and sharing knowledge in the developer community.

7. Documentation and References

- **MDN Web Docs:** A comprehensive resource for web developers, providing detailed documentation on web technologies.

- **DevDocs:** An offline documentation browser featuring instant search and a wide array of documentation sources.

- **GitHub Documentation:** Many libraries and frameworks host their documentation on GitHub, making it a valuable reference for developers.

8. Cloud Platforms

- **Amazon Web Services (AWS):** A cloud computing platform with a wide range of services for hosting, scaling, and managing applications.

- **Microsoft Azure:** Another major cloud platform offering a variety of services and tools for deploying and managing applications.

- **Google Cloud Platform (GCP):** Google's cloud offering with services for building and running applications.

These recommended tools and resources can help you become a more effective back-end developer, whether you're just starting or looking to expand your skill set. Be sure to explore them to find the ones that best suit your needs and preferences.

Conclusion

In this comprehensive guide, we've delved deep into the world of back-end development. We've covered a wide range of topics, from the fundamentals of back-end architecture and technologies to advanced concepts like microservices and serverless computing. Throughout this journey, we've aimed to provide you with a solid foundation and practical insights into building robust and scalable back-end systems.

As a back-end developer, you play a crucial role in ensuring the functionality, security, and performance of web applications. You are the backbone that supports the user-facing features, and your work directly impacts the user experience. Whether you're working with databases, APIs, or cloud services, your expertise is vital in delivering a seamless and reliable digital experience.

We hope this book has equipped you with the knowledge, tools, and best practices to excel in the field of back-end development. Remember that the technology landscape is continually evolving, so staying up-to-date with the latest trends and tools is essential. Keep exploring, learning, and pushing the boundaries of what's possible in back-end development.

Thank you for choosing this book as your guide. We appreciate your dedication to honing your back-end development skills. If you have any questions, feedback, or topics you'd like to explore further, please don't hesitate to reach out. We wish you the very best in your back-end development journey, and may your code always run smoothly!

Thank You!